THIRTY-ODD FEET
BELOW BELGIUM

An Affair of Letters
in the Great War 1915-1916

THIRTY-ODD FEET BELOW BELGIUM

An Affair of Letters
in the Great War 1915-1916

edited by
Arthur Stockwin

PARAPRESS LIMITED

Also published by Parapress Ltd:
Wren's Eye View by Stephanie Batstone
Sea Soldier, Letters and Journals of an Officer of Marines 1797–1813
Humanity Dick, the Story of Richard Martin, by Peter Phillips

© Arthur Stockwin 2005
ISBN-10: 1-898594-80-5
ISBN-13: 978-1898594-80-2

First published in the UK by
PARAPRESS LTD
The Basement
9 Frant Road
Tunbridge Wells
Kent TN2 5SD UK

British Library Cataloguing in Publication Data
A catalogue record of this book is available from the British Library.

Cover design by Mousemat Design Limited
www.mousematdesign.com

Wreath drawn by Harriet Buckley
www.harriart.co.uk

Typeset in Garamond by Helm Information Ltd

Print management by Sutherland Eve Production,
Tunbridge Wells, Kent, guyeve@theeves.fsnet.co.uk

Printed and bound in Great Britain
by Cromwell Press, Trowbridge, Wilts.

Contents

Illustrations

Preface

by PETER BARTON

It has been more than a quarter of a century since first I stood at the RE Grave on the Bellewaerde Ridge near Ypres in Belgian Flanders. On countless subsequent visits I have each time contemplated the fates of the dozen Royal Engineer Tunnellers commemorated on the memorial. Researching the story of their comrades – the small and tight-knit band of often entirely untrained (in military matters) mine managers, miners, sewer-drivers, and navvies, I have come to know a great deal of the life they led, the unique hazards faced, and also the grim deaths many suffered. But finding personal testimony has always been problematic. Even today avalanches of material about the surface war on the Western Front continue to appear almost daily, but the Tunnellers were an elite band, and few in number – a meagre 40,000 amongst an army of almost six million. Every contribution therefore, no matter how brief, is a jewel, adding another priceless gem to the crown of knowledge of this most clandestine of conflicts. In Arthur Stockwin's book we are not only offered a marvellous new collection, but one which presents an entirely fresh view of the underground war – the alien world in which Geoffrey Boothby spent the last year of his life.

Tunnellers' memoirs may be scarce, but collections of letters are yet more rare. The body of research into this most bizarre of struggles is immeasurably enriched by the correspondence between Geoffrey and Edith Ainscow. I have never come across such a revealing or affecting record – a record which is almost filmic in illustrating an all too transitory but intensely thrilling period in two young lives. The war made their distant liaison doubly exhilarating, and the outcome doubly tragic. Like

1

so many others, Geoffrey had hurried forward towards experiences of which he could never have dreamed. Being immediately attached to a Brigade Mining Section upon arrival in Belgium, he would soon have been fully conscious of the risk of permanently transferring to the Tunnellers, for theirs was by far the most treacherous undertaking on the Western Front; but his writing reveals a desire to join the Royal Engineers almost as strong as his yearnings to see Edith.

He protected her from his troglodyte world, shielding her from the primitive kill-or-be-killed struggle beneath no-man's-land. In hearing just a little – and that told in the unostentatious, cheerful style of the era, she may well have suffered more than he, for Geoffrey was busy, very busy, responsible for his men's lives, permanently excited by the novelty of war, learning the ever-developing 'tunnelling game', and grappling mentally and physically with continual danger. Working first at St Eloi and then Railway Wood – two veritable cauldrons of the underground war – he would have had far less time for periods of contemplation than his infantry colleagues.

For Edith and millions like her at home in Britain, however, there was just the waiting, the aching suspense, and the ever-present fear of bad news. By the beginning of 1916 casualty lists were already lengthy and the several offensives of the previous year had offered no signs of an end to the war, nor even a potential turning point; powerless families, especially the womenfolk, felt only the perpetual agony of uncertainty, and suffered a daily dread at the sound of the postman's footfall upon the garden path.

Despite being a part of this uneasy world, Edith's letters protect Geoffrey too, quite deliberately and very skilfully. They make him dream, they paint a picture of a warm and cherishing welcome; they are gently funny, optimistic, charitable, sympathetic, and make his youthful and apprehensive hints of passion sound noble. And, of course, they tantalise, which is possibly what Geoffrey needed and valued most to carry him away from the day-to-day barbarism – no word is more apt – of tunnelling. Written by one so young, they are no less than remarkable, and without a shadow of a doubt helped Geoffrey to cope with many perilous hours spent beneath the battlefields. To be able to witness the unfolding of a love story during this most symbolic of eras and under such unique circumstances – and by correspondence too – is almost more than the senses can take; the aura of suppressed and fearful hope is practically tangible. How lucky we of recent generations are to have enjoyed so many decades of peace.

The 177 Tunnelling Company War Diary shows us that Geoffrey Boothby today lies just a score of yards to the south of the Cross of Sacrifice on Bellewaerde Ridge, thirty feet down in the blue clay of Flanders; I have no doubt that Edith's photograph lies with him, in the tunic pocket closest to his heart.

Peter Barton,
co-author, *Beneath Flanders Fields*
April 2005

The Cross of Sacrifice, Bellewaerde Ridge

TELEPHONE
EDGBASTON 632.

Beechcroft,
1, Beech Lanes,
Birmingham.

29 . 3 . 16 .

Geoff, Dearest

I've got your
photo in front of me
just now and I
can hardly take my
eyes off it even to
write to you. I didn't
know anything could
make anybody so
happy. I'm afraid
I can't describe to you
~~know~~ what I think about
it. You'll just have
to imagine it. I'm
certain you'll be able to.

Introduction

On 6th April 1990 I found the key to a wooden chest in my father's house in Birmingham. My mother had died nearly seven years earlier and he, aged 86, had been taken into a nursing home. I was clearing the Victorian house that they had bought in 1934, around the time of their marriage.

When I opened the chest, I found in it a cardboard box full of letters between my mother and a young officer in the Great War, called Geoffrey Boothby. I had had no knowledge of their relationship and could hardly believe what I had discovered.[1]

The letters told the story of a love affair between two young people, cut short by war. Most of it was conducted by writing. When Geoffrey left for his training camp in Dorset in early February 1915, he and Edith had been in each other's company – as Geoffrey later calculated – for a total of about four incomplete days.

Their relationship, uncertain at first, developed, deepened, went through inevitable ups and downs, and intensified into love. Plainly they knew each other far better at the end than at the beginning. But all they could do was to write to each other and send the occasional present. Circumstances prevented them meeting on Geoffrey's home leaves, and indeed they were never to meet again. When Edith wrote him her last letter, Geoffrey was already dead: blown up by a German mine in a tunnel at Railway Wood near Ieper (Ypres) in Flanders on 28th April 1916.

Charles Geoffrey Boothby was born on 13th December 1894, and so was one of that narrow generation fated to celebrate their 21st

Edith, Gladys and Arthur Ainscow as children.

birthdays in the trenches. In Geoffrey's case he was "thirty odd feet below the surface of Belgium & somewhat nearer the Huns than the people in the trenches". Edith Ainscow was born on 9th January 1898, and celebrated her 18th birthday soon after Geoffrey's 21st. At the time of their meeting they both lived in the Birmingham area with their respective parents. Edith's father was a general practitioner, running a broadly working-class practice in Birmingham,[2] while Geoffrey's father worked for a firm of manufacturing chemists in West Bromwich.[3] Geoffrey had no brothers or sisters, but he had a cousin called Herbert who is mentioned occasionally in the letters, although he is never named. Edith was the youngest of three children (a fourth had died in infancy), together with her sister Gladys and brother Arthur. Arthur was clearly one of Geoffrey's close friends, and went to the war at about the same time. But he was lucky enough to be posted to Mesopotamia in the Royal Flying Corps, though later he was wounded at Gallipoli and at one stage also he was in Egypt. He figures quite frequently in the letters.

I am not sure how Edith and Geoffrey first met, but Arthur may well have introduced them.

Geoffrey was admitted to the University of Birmingham to read Medicine in the autumn of 1914, but seems only to have stayed a few weeks,[4] before going to officer school at Camberley. Edith visited him there on at least one occasion. According to his service record, he was confirmed as an officer in the Regular Army (South Staffordshire Regiment) for the period of the war on 24th December 1914.[5] He left for Bovington Camp at Wool in Dorset at the beginning of February 1915.

Between then and December 1915 only the letters from Geoffrey to Edith have survived, but there seems to be a full run of correspondence from December until the following May. Geoffrey's earlier letters are full of bravado and a sense of adventure. While based at his training camp, he rides on a series of ramshackle motor bikes, which he falls off rather regularly. Once (later, in France) he rides a horse, which scares him even more. One evening he and some of his fellow officers take out a group of actresses who, he assures Edith, "are not as black as they are painted", and he wishes she had been there too.

In his first letter from France, he assures her that he has never been more excited in his life. But after a few weeks the mood begins to change, as he finds himself in the trenches (and later, tunnels) in the middle of a genuine shooting war. He is seconded from the South Staffs Regiment to the Royal Engineers and is engaged in the actual digging. In a letter dated September he tells of his first experience of seeing a fellow officer killed – "one of the best officers in the regiment". He uses this to sound off against those "plausible youths" who have managed to stay back in Britain and he fears are "snapping up" the girls. This is the time when Edith is just about to begin at university, and he pleads with her not to read science, which would be "an absolute catastrophe", but to study for a "MEDICAL CAREER". This she duly did. Some oblique hints follow that he was being left behind in his career by those who stayed at home; this later happened to Arthur as well, with corrosive effects. In February he airily doubts whether he will ever take up a dental or medical career, since "it would be such an age before I could qualify".

A letter from Geoff in March speaks jocularly about his recently taken photo, which does not do justice to his moustache. But then a few sentences later, and without warning, he writes: "Nearly all my friends in the Staffords have been killed in the fighting round Ypres a few weeks ago. It's a horribly sad thing how many friendships have been made and broken by this war. But it does make one proud to be an Englishman, when one knows how unselfishly one's friends go west. However, the subject will depress you." As time goes on jocularity becomes more and more a cover for edginess and just occasionally the intense strain shows through in jagged fashion. But the idea that he should not be there in those appalling conditions doing his duty for his country never seems to enter his head. Nevertheless, there is a giveaway line in a letter dated April: "Other people's troubles don't interest us at all round here." The Germans are referred to by some well-known uncomplimentary nouns, but also as "the unmentionables" and "the abominables".[6] But those back home who managed to escape war service are, if anything, even greater targets of his wrath. He also expresses impatience with arrogant Guards officers who are "the sons of dukes", while finding some of their kind reasonably acceptable.

Edith, meanwhile, provides him with girlish fantasies of living in some rural English Eden with dog and parrot in her "dream cottage". He thinks he can improve on the dream. She sends him romantic poems, which he learns by heart. She writes of reading a book by the American, William Osler, about how students should deal with the problems of living.[7] To contemporary taste its advice is unbearably pompous and preachy, but she says it makes her feel good (as does *Omar Khayyam*!), but then "I don't agree with it a scrap." In her letters, as in his, there is the jokeyness that masks anxiety, both about the security of their relationship and about the danger that he is in. She is, after all, a girl of seventeen and then eighteen, who has just left school and is starting at university. One can only wonder at her real thoughts, when she has to write cheerful letters to him knowing full well in her heart of hearts that his chances of survival are probably small.

The correspondence is spiced with some delicious period slang. Things are "topping", "ripping", they are "bucked" to receive each other's letters, among Edith's fellow students there is "one real live occifer" (slang for 'officer'). Very occasionally we come across expressions which today would be regarded as 'non-PC', an example of our own period slang. Once or twice there is implicitly anti-Semitic language, for instance when Geoffrey remarks that it was "Jewish" of him to seek to retrieve his torch during a gun battle in one of the tunnels. But this is rare, and the letters, despite occasional spelling mistakes, are highly literate, even literary.

They were, of course, not meant to be published, and even now that nine decades have passed I feel some qualms about doing so. But they are such wonderful examples of youthful humanity, faced with the horrors of one of the most vicious wars ever fought. That is surely sufficient to justify making them available for people born long after the events they describe.

Notes

1. See Epilogue, subheading 'Discovery', for a fuller account of how I found the letters, and with what effect.
2. James Ainscow and his wife Mary both hailed from Lancashire, but he had done his medical training at the University of Edinburgh, graduating in 1906, when Edith was already eight years old.
3. According to the 1901 census, Geoffrey's father, Charles, was born at Stockport in Cheshire; his wife Alice was born at Newington, and Geoffrey himself was born in Brixton. In 1901 the family was living at Leyton in Essex. I am grateful to Anna Jo Righton for this information. It seems that they moved to West Bromwich only about three years before the events described in the letters. Geoffrey plainly regarded the "awful" Black Country as in part responsible for his father's breakdown in health.
4. He is listed in the University of Birmingham Virtual War Memorial. See firstworldwar@bham.ac.uk .
5. National Archives file WO339/5068.
6. A word also used once or twice for his particular *bêtes noires*, those back home who had managed to evade war service.
7. William Osler, *A Way of Life, An Address to Yale Students Sunday evening, April 20th, 1913*. London, Constable and Company Ltd., 1913. Osler was perhaps the best known medical doctor of the first few years of the twentieth century.

The Letters

- transcribed with the original spelling and punctuation -

4th South Staffords
Bovington Camp.
Wool
Dorset.
7/2/15.

Dear Edith,

You know my address now, so you've no excuse for not writing, & why on earth didn't you come to see Arthur off, I was on his train by accident. You see, I had a bit of a rush on Wednesday morning, in fact I had to dress & do half my packing in ten minutes. I was rather roughly awakened by the arrival of the taxi which was to take me to the station. I did the dressing etc in time & got to S. Hill just in time to see my train going out. The guard would be in sulphurous quarters by now if thoughts could kill. However, I found your brother & Collins on the next train & that made up for it. We travelled down to Southampton together.

I don't know what sort of a place Arthur has struck, but I've got to a hole miles beyond nowhere, infinity, in fact

6th South Staffords
Bovington Camp
Wool
Dorset
7/2/15

Dear Edith,

You know my address now, so you've no excuse for not writing, & why on earth didn't you come to see Arthur off, I was on his train by accident. You see, I had a bit of a rush on Wednesday morning, in fact I had to dress and do half my packing in ten minutes. I was rather roughly awakened by the arrival of the taxi which was to take me to the station. I did the dressing etc. in time & got to S. Hill* just in time to see my train going out. The guard would be in sulphurous quarters by now if thoughts could kill. However, I found your brother & Collins on the next train & that made up for it. We travelled down to Southampton together.

I don't know what sort of a place Arthur has struck, but I've got to a hole miles beyond nowhere, infinity, in fact the limit. Mud, huts, desolation & Tommies, nothing else unless I include the bugles which go all night & day, mostly with wrong notes.

Almost as soon as I got here I was pounced upon & innoculated, & ever since I've been having a – er – devil of a time, arm about twice as big as Sandow's & a ghastly attack of something like flu. In spite of it all my cast iron constitution has survived it & I am about to take my platoon to church for the second time today. The evening show should be pretty good, the chaplain said there was going to be a cinematograph present, & though I haven't been to church for two years, I'm quite looking forward to it: converted by cinema, sounds rather well, what do you think?

There are fourteen officers in a hut here, our hut being distinguished by the possession of a piano & a gramophone, also the mud in ours is not more than half an inch deep.

---

* Snow Hill Station, one of the two main railway stations in Birmingham at that time.

Glad to hear you're going to use my hanky as a scarf. Yours came in most useful in a most unromantic way. I lost my own on the way down (not on purpose) & as my luggage didn't arrive till the next day I had to use yours. Good thing it wasn't scented, since I've been able to have it washed and added it to my collection (which now amounts to the huge sum of two.) I asked ——— (censor)* where she got that scent. It's French & has an unpronouncable name. Sorry I can't give fuller particulars.

Guess I'd better shut up now. Don't forget a letter would not come amiss.

Cheero!

Geoff.

In case you know more than a dozen Geoffs my other name's Boothby. I guess you said "what a cheek!" as soon as you started to read this letter.

Once more

Cheero!

8th Bn. S. Staffords
Bovington Camp
Wool
Dorset
13/2/15

Dear Edith,

Your letter tickled me immensely, especially the nasty knocks; you're several up now, I'm afraid I can't keep up with you in these personalities. I haven't had any photos from Arthur, so I haven't seen the one, in which I am so conspicuous by my absence, please send some on, if you can get any.

You were quite wrong about the 'mysterious she' seeing me off, I'm not QUITE so conceited as to expect people to drag themselves out at 7.30, unless it was to have the pleasure of seeing the last of me. No, alas!

---

* Jokes about censorship are standard fare in these letters.

Had I caught the train I should have gone alone and unwept for, no flag wagging, no nothing. Wouldn't it have been sad, especially on an empty stomach? However, enough of this gloom.

I'm beginning to recover from the depression under which I spent the first few days here, in fact I'm quite enjoying myself in spite of not having had a proper bath since I've been here. The country's not half bad except the spot on which the camp is situated. It's frightfully quiet, one of those places I used to sigh for when I was a nice quiet boy, that is to say about eight months ago, not a house for miles. Wool, the nearest village, consists of a public house, station, post office and two shops-of-all-trades: I visited one this afternoon & came back laden with a haversack-full of spoil ranging from boot dubbin to Turkish delight (made in England). I'm in a gorgeous state of stodge or complete indifference to food by now.

By the way have you met my cousin since the night we went to the theatre? You'll find him good fun when he comes out of his shell. He's booked already, but that doesn't matter much. I'll be consumed with jealousy if I hear you've been going to the Picture House with him more than five times a week. Red haired people are noted for their jealousy and bad temper.

You shall have a button as soon as I've got a store in, you see I didn't think it worth getting any while I was in B'ham, I only know two girls worth knowing in that city. I had a most embarrassing experience the other day. The Captain of our company was giving the men a lecture on giving away buttons and badges when they get to France. I was quite enjoying his description of the bewitching females they would meet there when suddenly I noticed several of the Tommies looking rather intently at my tunic. It didn't take me long to discover that one of my badges was missing. As I was seated in state facing the men I felt rather small. Anyway I had the grace to blush. Therefore you must be patient & wait till I get some buttons from the tailor, I don't want to have another such experience.

The piano still exists & still gives good music. The owner is a fine player & his voice is quite perfect. He got a £50 scholarship to Cambridge for singing, so you see he's some good. When ever he sings anything at all sentimental my mind switches on to people I know with blue eyes and gorgeous hair (quite real) & I feel a curious feeling under the solar plexus. I think savages and uncivilized peoples are quite right in making the tummy the seat of the emotions, don't you? But perhaps I shouldn't ask you such things, though I know you'll pass some facetious remark on the above; however, I'll let it stand. I'll send Phyllis your love as you asked, & please write soon.

Cheero!

Geoff.

8th Bn. S. Staffords
Wool
Dorset
19/2/15

Dear Edith,

A million thanks for the scarf, I can quite imagine you worked pretty hard at it to get it done so soon. Hope it isn't one you started ages ago for some "other". Anyway, whether it is or it isn't it's ripping of you to send it to me, & the fact that you've worn it (not as a body belt) adds 100% to its value as you expected.

As for the Harlene, well the last I saw of it was in the stove, I tried to press it on each of the subs in this hut in turn but they didn't seem to appreciate it, of course that's what you meant me to do with it, wasn't it. I didn't suppose for a moment it was meant for me, my moustache is QUITE visible now, thanks. After trying all the officers in the regiment without success, I put the thing on the stove to see whether the heat would grow lightening whiskers on the cork. No success again. By the way how did YOU get to know & also get possession of the magic potion? Hope the hair, which I mentioned apparently pleasingly in my last, was not the result of patient and judicious applications *cotidie*. See, I know some Latin, I guess I was as good or bad a swot as you were at one time. Thank God we've both got over it.

Was I very subdued at Camberley? I'm often like that at first, it isn't exactly shyness; you see I thought I hadn't a ghost of a chance, when Carr was on the scene & it's only waste of time to butt in on such occasions. You should have seen me grinding my teeth with envy, when I had to walk alone on that last evening at Camberley, you'd have been rather tickled. In fact I had to have my molars repaired the next day the damage was so great. Heigho! What a life!

Arthur has just sent me the photos, so I can now appreciate, as I did not before the photos came, your rude remarks about my obliterated features. It was very unsporting of you to say such things, when they were not even on the photo to defend themselves. Never mind, I gave you tit for tat with the ill timed remark about red hair and jealousy, so we'll call it quits. The later remarks in my letter were for once in a way true, so you needn't have taken a pinch of salt (or Harlene) with them.

Why this question about girls smoking? Of course I agree with it. As I ventured to state at your house, I think properly done it is a most graceful operation when performed by the ever graceful feminine. (Quite good that bit, what!) But there, you told me at Camberley, when I was trying to find out as much as possible about you in my subdued way, that you didn't smoke, so I suppose you don't agree with my above remark, which is most sad (I mean the fact that you don't agree.) If you've taken to smoking in your swotting hours as well as writing top-hole letters to undeserving subalterns, I hope you won't have got as far as a pipe by the time I come home again. Stick to Turkish and you'll be alright, my dear; De Reske for preference.

By the way Arthur told me Alta Gibb's address, & also said she would be pleased to get a P.C. from me re the photos. As I'm perfectly sure she wouldn't, what had I better do?

I've sent for the buttons, so you can begin to expect them and get the lavender ready; vile stuff lavender, frousy [*sic*] & reminiscent of early Victorian days coupled with hermetically sealed windows.

Yes, it would be a most sensible plan to come to Swanage and Bournemouth & alone, but it's no use coming in the summer as all the young subs will be dead by then, come now and see if I'm as subdued as I was at Camberley. My heart goes pit-a-pat at the thought of it, I can't feel it as I've been innoculated in the chest, but still I can pretty well assume it's pit-a-patting, you see it always does.

Well, I guess I'll become a drought & dry up. Sorry I can't manage any compliments to finish up with but as I couldn't possibly do justice, I'll leave my feeble efforts unsaid.

Cheero!

Geoff.

Not much news in this letter, sorry, but I'll give it you in large chunks in my next, which will I hope be in answer to the letter you're about to write me.

8th Bn. S. Staffords.
Bovington
Wool
3/3/15

Dear Edith,

This note to ask what's up. What have I done, why this silence? I'm jumping to all sorts of hasty conclusions. Have you eloped with my cousin, who hasn't answered my last letter either? Have I offended on the smoking question, or have you unearthed some compromising incident from the depths of my shady past? Two other theories remain, either you've taken to swotting or you're too bored to write. Which of all these is it? I enclose buttons as payment for information. I don't quite know how to continue this letter until I get the tip from you. You see if the first conclusion is right, you'll never get the letter, & if any of the others are correct, you wouldn't deign to read any more, so I don't see how I'm to go on. In spite of my grief at not getting anything from you, I've been having a fairly good time. Since I wrote last I've done several mad things, the maddest of which have been a bathe in the sea & an adventurous voyage on the channel in a cockleshell boat, in which I had to row all the time to keep off sea sickness.

Also I went to Bournemouth last Saturday, awfully nice place after this confounded camp. By a happy fluke I met Pelham, one of the fellows you met at Camberley. He, Arthur and I were more or less inseparable. Considering that he was stationed at Aldershot, when we left Camberley, it was quite a shock to meet him.

As I haven't had time to write a five page letter I'll dry up and hope you'll write soon & let me know the worst.

Cheero!

Geoff.

8th Bn. S. Staffords
Bovington
Wool
29/3/15

Dear Edith,

Please excuse pencil, but it's more convenient for writing in front of the fire.

Glad to hear I may write to you still, I thought from your last & the reference to the "Punch" article that you were getting bored with writing. However!

Sorry to say I can't get any Easter leave, none going in this regt for some reason. Damnable, isn't it!

The one topic that holds me at present (except the people I have to think of at Brum of course) is motor cycles. You see I've just been reckless enough to buy one. New Hudson 3½, three speed and free engine. It's an absolute ripper, second hand but only a year old.

Incidentally, I've overdrawn my money at Cox's, but still that's a detail.

So far, I've only had one accident. No damage. I merely found myself suddenly in a cul-de-sac & wasn't able to stop before a big gate stopped me. However, as I mentioned above, no damage.

Wish I could have the pleasure of scorching about with you on the back. It would be suicide for both of us but perhaps we would have some exciting times before we came off.

Still I may have some practice down here with luck, in taking passengers I mean; who knows?

Nothing much happens here out of the ordinary now-a-days, same sort of rubbish every day. Did I tell you I'm in command of a platoon at present? I've had it for about a month.

My moustache, I'm almost certain, is progressing, perhaps motor cycling will help it on. I've already shaken out a filling with the vibration.

I'm going to bed now so Good Night!

& write soon

Cheero!

Geoff.

8th (Service) Battn
South Staffordshire Regt.
Wool
3/5/15

Dear Edith,

A million apologies but no excuses. Excuses are no good in the Army, what! What! I believe I am about to see your estimable brother's cheery countenance. Next Saturday at Bournemouth I'll endeavour to keep him out of mischief. With his consent we're to stay the night and have a general bust up.

Motor cycling aint all cakes and ale. At present my bike is undergoing repairs which will come to roughly £6! And I've escaped narrowly with my life. The bally thing "seized up" as they call it, & by rights I should have sailed over the handle bars while going at forty m/hr. I didn't, my infernal luck as usual. As it is I have escaped with a scratch & remain to pay the bill. Heigho, what a life!

We are now in tents, just above Lulworth Cove. Topping place, high on the cliffs & as fresh as anything. We've had some broiling weather too & two bathing parades, which were very nice but for the fact that all the fair maidens of the village assembled on the cliffs, which was rather embarrassing, since both men & officers bathe – er, well, the government haven't issued costumes to us yet. Still I'm getting fairly blush proof. Got an approach to a bath too, which is quite a consideration.

If I don't get to the front soon, I think I'll try & get a weekend leave home, not until the bike's done though, I'm not going to waste any time walking to and from stations this time. Not going to try taking passengers yet awhile. Tried one astride without feeling at all steady; of course, it was only a brother officer, what would have happened if a damsel had been on 'side saddle' G. O. K. [*God only knows*]

I wonder if you'll write to me, please make a good old effort.

Cheero!
Geoff.

LIST OF ENTRANTS 1914
c/c = Cycle car, s/c = sidecar

P Grout	(8 Morgan c
FC Wasley	(8 Zenith s
A Stevens	(3½ Zeni
WW Moore	(4 Douglas s
CE Hokes	(3½ Sunbea
D Hawkes	(10 Victor c
E Kickham	(2½ Dougl
CHR Norrington	(6 Enfield s
PH Mathews	(4 Nort
AL Clayden	(10 AC c
FG Ball	(2½ Dougl
H Greaves	(8 Enfield s
WH Rudge	(3½ W
L Martin	(10 Singer c
HN Walker	(2½ Dougl
T Heath	(6 Sunbeam s
G Brough	(3½ Brou
C Hooper	(10 Douglas c
H Petty	(3½ Brou
W Eggington	(8 Enfield s
PB Phillips	(2½ Dougl
R Davis	(8 Charter Lea
W McKeggie	(3½ Brou
PA Stone	(8 Morgan c
MSP King	(10 AC c

The role of motorcycles in the war featured heav in the motorcycling press. These dispatch riders, attached to the Royal Engineers, pose with a New Hudson V-twin in December 1914.

The type of Hudson motorcycle that gave Geoffrey much trouble.
By kind permission of the Morton Media Group.

8th (Service) Battn
South Staffordshire Regt
Flower Down Camp
Winchester
3/6/15

Dear Edith,

I write to tell you that I'm probably coming home on leave next weekend 11th to 15th, so don't be surprised if I turn up to see how things in general are going. I don't expect you'll deign to know me after my lapse in writing, but I'll try my luck. Quite a lot of out of the way incidents have occurred since I last wrote. First pray observe the address. Winchester, yes we moved over here about a week ago. At least we started to move; took four days & a half to accomplish the march and slept in the open every night, no tents, no nothing, just a valise & a couple of blankets. Mon dieu, the dew! (Please notice pun.) Thank God we didn't have any rain.

Another item of interest (to me anyway) is that we have spent forty-eight hours in trenches. Rather tiring job as we, the horficers, only got about three hours sleep the whole time. Myself and my platoon were attached to the Royal Engineers the first night. Our job was to carry devil's machines, technically called the cheval de frise,[1] vulgarly known as barbed wire entanglements out in front of the trenches. Complete silence is supposed to reign, but this becomes rather trying when a whip of barbed wire wraps itself round your legs or you fall into the enemy's trenches, generally for some reason flat on the little Mary or tummy. Both these pleasant little interludes fell to my lot. I got to bed at 2 a.m., & was roused again at 3.30 a.m. since they have a playful habit in the trenches of "standing to arms" at this hour. This consists of the officer going round and kicking his men gently till they stand. I'm afraid I had to shut my ears that morning.

I have acquired another motor bike, older but faster than my New Hudson. It's not exactly safe to take passengers on it. It's changed hands four times in 3 months, & every owner has had an uncomfortable smash on it. My last victim was a drunken Tommy who's still in hospital recovering from drink and a bad stunning. There was another victim with him but he was only knocked flat, winded & bruised somewhat. Your dearest & best belovèd escaped with a very bad shaking up & five minutes unconsciousness. Quite exciting what! All right now, only rather sore down one side. An awfully sporting girl got out of her car & rendered first aid to the Tommy. As we were waiting for about an hour for the ambulance, I had a long conversation which must have led to my speedy recovery. Tommy unconscious all the time though, which rather marred things. He's getting better now.

My cousin, who I'm jealous to observe seems to interest you, is at present safely away in Sussex where he is being coached to get into Woolwich. He's going into the Royal Engineers, regulars, not K's [*Kitchener's*] army. At present he seems to be particularly interested in a girls' school which is next door to the place where he himself is imbibing knowledge. He has of course left K. E. S. [*King Edward's School, Birmingham*]

You'll be sorry to hear, if you believe me, that I haven't written to "the other" for about five weeks. Guess I'm too slack for anything.

Well

   Cheero, Blue Eyes!
     Yr loving
      Geoff.
       Bow Wow!

8th (Service) Battn.
South Staffordshire Regt.
Flower Down
Winchester
19/6/15

Golden Locks (whew!)

A ghastly disaster overtook me during my leave. This bolt from the blue arrived on Saturday night in the shape of a telegram to say I had to return here by the Monday morning for firing a new course. I flatter myself that my language was that of a connoisseur, original & to the point. Nevertheless I had to come back all the same.

I didn't get your very formal letter till I got back but I was coming to Beechcroft on Sunday night in any case; as it was I had to leave Brum at midday. I would have you know that my visit to you was at great physical inconvenience since Fortune & motor cycling had dealt rather roughly with me on my journey from Winchester to Brum. But now I'm merely grousing for any possible amount of hurts would be hopelessly over compensated for by the fact that I was going to see YOU. Very nice, what!

To put it shortly this is what happened. I was puffing along in the dark on the last twenty five miles of my journey when suddenly my front wheel began to wobble. As it was dark I couldn't see the cause, which didn't matter much since the next moment I was sliding along the road with the bike on top of me, both bike and I having turned round in the process & facing the direction I'd come along. Well I picked myself up & found all was well but I was considerably knocked about (here you begin to weep please). I drove into Brum feeling very miserable and shaky. Here I had to get off to find the way. Putting my hand down to my side I was horrified to find (repress the shriek) to find my breeches soaked in blood. At least a good patch was. Of course, my leg began to hurt then thereby showing how powerful the imagination can become. When I got home I found a large area of leg devoid of cuticle & several very deep but short gashes where the stones had made themselves evident. This of course kept me in the house all the time I was at home; it healed pretty quickly though and now it's only a little stiff.

So I didn't see the Other One, as you may have suspected, daren't in fact, not having written for two months.

I expect to get leave again soon since my last was cut down so much. Next time I'll come straight to Beechcroft so's to be quite certain of seeing you. Heigho! Woe is me! Etc Etc.

Yours in sighs, Blue Eyes!

Love

Geoff.

Post scriptum

I wrote to you at the beginning of this week, & naturally forgot to post the letter. Discovered it among some papers this morning.

Geoff.

P.P.S. I was very worried during my leave by thoughts of a certain corporal I ran over some days ago. When I came home I heard that the man was on the point of kicking the bucket from concussion. Very luckily for me the man has recovered. Lord! I was glad to hear he was better!

8th (Service) Battn.
South Staffordshire Regt.
Flower Down Camp
Winchester.
11/7/15

Blue Eyes,

The time of all times has arrived! We go to the front at any moment now. How long this "any moment" touch will last God only knows. We were informed at the beginning of the week that we had to be ready to move on Sunday or any subsequent date decided upon. Well the first day of the "any moment" period has arrived & up to now we've heard nothing. The Colonel tells us that we must be prepared to march off any time at two hours notice, so we're in for a time of suspense until we get the order.

Unlike many regts. we are going straight to the trenches, so says that unreliable dame, Mme. Rumour, because the artillery are being given live shells, which would not happen if we were going to a base to finish training as usually happens. I only just scraped into the position of platoon commander the day we got the news. Jolly lucky, as all supernumary [*sic*] officers are staying at home in the 11th Battn.

My Lord! The crossing! I shall be so considerate as to feed the poor little fishes with the dinner which I don't want, or rather, which my little Mary won't want. You say you're coming to Bournemouth sometime this week. Wire me as soon as you get there, where you're staying & if I'm still in England, I'll endeavour to come over.[2]

This week has been a lively one for me.

Last Sunday, had a day on the river at Maidenhead, & did a hundred mile ride to get there and back.

Monday. Theatre Royal, Winchester

Tuesday. Afternoon & evening in London

Wed. slack

Thursday. Theatre. Southampton.

Arrived back at 3 AM.

Friday do do do [*ditto ditto ditto*].

Saturday do do do 4 AM.

"Ha! Ha!" You say, "why three times to the theatre in S'hampton, & why these shocking hours?"

Well, my dear, since my heart is filled with sadness I will confess.

I have had a little affair with an actress. Now don't tear this up having read so far. I haven't had anything to do with girls for six months, in other words since that night at Beechcroft. I thought as I only had a limited time in Eng. I ought to improve the shining hour. So four others, who were going out and myself each secured girls and formed a limited supper company.

I won't bore you with descriptions, except that actresses are not as black as they're painted, you yourself would have enjoyed the company immensely. Also they, at least these, neither drop their aitches nor speak in an affected "high class" way (which is worse), in other words they were as ourselves. Of course there are companies and companies, but I confess this was a bit of an eye opener for me. I always used to imagine they were all out & outers & respectable ones were only to be found in books. Some girls! Most sincerely I wish you'ld [*sic*] been there, you'ld have had a fine time.

You say you've qualified as a divinity, so please forgive once more. After all, I <u>have</u> written and told you all about it.

If you can recover in time, please write by return, I may be dead tomorrow or at any rate wishing I was aboard a trooper.

I'm not the fickle villain you no doubt by now believe me to be, but "Eat, drink and be merry, for tomorrow_____."

Cheero, Darling.

Geoff.

[posted to Birmingham, forwarded to an address in Bournemouth. The first letter with a censor's stamp on the envelope]

8th S. Staffords
B.E.F.
France.
[Postmarked 26 July 15]

Darling

You now have a real live "lonely soldier somewhere in France". Only he's not very lonely. Also it's beastly conceited to imagine you hadn't got several others. Let us say "another – er – boy in France". Also please forgive him, if he's not feeling depressed or homesick. He's not. Never been more excited in his life before.

You see we're waiting 'way back behind the firing line for our turn for a little amateur scrapping. Knowing you as I do (having been in your company for, I believe, a period of four incomplete days all told), knowing you as I do, I repeat, I feel certain you will condone this temporary lapse from continuous heartbrokeness [*sic*] under which I am supposed to stagger, whenever absent from No 1. Beeches Rd.

Only once have I strafed the Germans for bringing me out here to make myself a nuisance to themselves, & that was when I got your telegram, which got here yesterday by the way. Two days longer in England and _____ . [*blank, not censored*]

However, it's not much use kicking up a row about it, Kitchener's not one of my intimates, so I'll have to pass it over this time & qualify as a divinity by your method, – forgiveness.

To come to some real news, we've had a mixed sort of time since we came out. Easy billets & some very mouldy marching.

The men stuck it damn well. We had a long march under the most trying conditions for some of them especially those with tender feet. The notorious pavé or cobbled roads are the last word. As usual our regt. come off easily best in marching having two fall out against eighty two of another regt. Some boys, ours. Grousing all the while, but sticking to it like Trojans. We are now within sound of the big guns & sight of aerial scraps, which seem to occur every evening. Haven't seen one brought down yet.

We have great fun getting the inhabitants to execute our wishes. I haven't been stumped yet, though I can't understand a word they answer. We have been issued with a blue book of useful sentences which strange to relate ARE useful. I stride into a new billet, rap out my stock phrase, *vide* book & thenceforward carry on with patchy sentences or scattered words. Works, though, you'd be surprised at the powers of understanding these people have.

Well, I suppose we're fixtures here for a month or two. Happy Days!

Cheero, Blue Eyes,

Geoff.

8th S. Staffs
B.E.F.
11/8/15

Dear Girl,

Your suggestion that I should tell you how many fair charmers I had writing to me in exchange for the number of lonely soldiers with whom you corresponded is scarcely fair.

I made the last confession, it's up to you now. And not to make any conditions either, leave it to my discretion, as to whether I make two confessions to your one or not. However, I'll promise not to be too discreet if your answer proves unfavourable to myself.

Since I last wrote we have moved about a bit, & have experienced shell fire & a very haphazard sort of rifle fire.

We lived in a district for a week that was apparently a dumping place for German shells, they come from time to time all over the show, but never nearer to your best belovéd (or rather one of them) than one field away. Still they gave quite a zest to lunch in the open. It was on one of these occasions that I got your letter. Their favourite time for shelling, however, was early dawn, a most dastardly time, for it is hard to conceive a more unpleasant experience than that of waking in the early hours of the morning & finding your burberry has deserted you in your hour of need & left you like an icicle, especially as the row doesn't allow you to recall the goddess of repose for at least an hour and a half. Heigho! How the world ill uses us (in our own estimation.)

Now I've had my little grouse, I'll endeavour to bear up & become less dull.

We are back in a rest camp. Back to the land of clothes off at night! of baths! (in tubs in a brewery, where they don't like us to use soap, as the horses have to drink the water after we've finished with it. Fact!) Sorry to say I was so inconsiderate to the wretched equines as to saponify the water; however, I'm not the only culprit. Back to the land of sleeping bags, quiet o'nights & regular posts!

(By the way, if this letter stinks of carbolic, when you get it, it's because a _____ed R.A.M.C. man has inadvertently sprayed me by mistake for a bundle of old clothes or a hut or something. I can't quite gather which.)

In case you are drawing a reverse conclusion, I beg to state that I & the others are thoroughly enjoying ourselves over here. The life is so gorgeously happy-go-lucky, that one cannot but be in good spirits. Hours don't count, we are just as liable to get up at 3 A.M. as to go to bed at that hour, & as for grub, we're all getting perfect epicures.

One black spot alone remains. I have a continually recurring picture in my apology for a brain of yourself accompanied by 2nd Lt x.y.z. on the river at Christchurch. It must be my red hair. Which latter by the way is nowhere more than an eighth of an inch long, owing to the prevalent fashion out here among young subalterns of looking as much like convicts as possible. We go so far as to call one another by numbers. I am No. 70.

Well, I must endeavour to curb my drivelling & be sporting enough to wish you a pleasant time with that scoundrel x.y.z.

Cheero!

Yrs.

No. 70.

26/8/15*

Dear Edith,

Thanks awfully for the cigarettes. Glad to see you remember the ones I like. Thanks also for the confession. To the winds with Discretion! I have one other correspondent, my actress having ceased to write some time ago, or rather I did the ceasing. Fickle Villain!

That, I think, ought to close the subject.

I have had a somewhat lively time of late. To begin with we've been in the trenches themselves for some days. We were first in the support trenches for three days where all was quiet & peaceful. True, shells did burst considerably nearer than a field away & sent rather unfriendly

---

* *Sic*, but see below

looking lumps of hot metal into the trench, but no one was hurt, so we achieved our little bit in making them waste a few hundred pounds worth of munitions.

We then went up to the fire trenches, two hundred yards ahead, & about eighty yards from the Despicable One. Here things were comparatively quiet, but only comparatively. We had several quite bracing incidents of [*sic*] the trenches. We are going to requisition for motor cycles among other things. Several other Brigades have provided their mining officers with them. We live at Bde H. Q, when the Batt is in the trenches. Some job! Got it four days ago, & am now doing a short course of mining with the R.E. Twenty four hours in the trenches & forty eight out! The rest of the Batt are in the trenches now and I'm in luxurious quarters. Piano, spring beds, peace & quiet! Just doing my 48 hours spell.

26/8/15

Note above date. Too lazy to finish letter on 24th.

I have had my first experience of the back of a horse. Rode into — — with Hare, who as transport officer does not go into the trenches.

God! When the beast started to trot! I had a hell of time – till I managed to get into the swing & not bounce like a sack to each movement of the horse. We rode twelve miles altogether & I had every kind of equestrian motion, & even jumped a ditch without falling off.

The creature got away with me once too. Picture me, bumping away, feet and knees all over the place. I didn't cuddle its neck though.

Today I went a motor cycle ride over roads which were consistently as bad as the Bovington Wool road. My behind was sore enough when I started, when I got back, whew!

Last night there was a wire to say that three of the officers of the RE Coy to which I am attached raked in one DSO & 2 Military Crosses, between them for bagging the charge out of a German mine which they struck.

Cheero

Boothby [*sic*]

8th. S.S.R.
14/9/15

Dear Edith,

You're a buck! Thanks awfully for the papers & that ripping letter, which I received a few days late owing to the various peregrinations and passages upon which I have been bent for some time past. In more vulgar language, I've been moving about some lately.

At last I'm settled, pro tem. Anyway. Until further notice I am attached to the 172 Coy R.E. for tunneling duty. You see my Brigade Mining Section & another have been amalgamated & placed at the disposal of the 172 Coy.

As I believe I told you before, this is right in my line, good billets, piano, good grub and every inconvenience eliminated. Also 24 hours in trenches & 48 out. Use of motor cycles, & horses (if we want 'em).

By the way I have just read "Freckles". It is one of those which may be entered in the category – I don't know how to spell it – of 'pretty'. Why did you want me to read it? I can only imagine to wish to picture our belovéd selves in the principals. I do believe you'd like me to come home handless to increase the supposed likeness in the boy, you bloodthirsty scoundrel! Or is the feminine of scoundrel scoundreless or even scoundrelle?

I must say the resemblence [*sic*] in the girl is far more perfect, – ahem – er – that last remark in itself deserves a good long letter in answer.

So now you are a woman of affairs (business affairs, I mean.) Hope you have regained courage to go back &, in your own words, "do some useful work with the men in the Council House".

My bike is still together & is at present undergoing a rest cure in a shed, unless the mater is emulating your example and riding it on the lawn. Poor mater! I guess she's rather lonely. Thank Heaven she's moving out of that awful Black Country & has taken a little cottage near Redditch.

I'm afraid W. Bromwich hasn't been a lucky spot for our family, during the three years we were there. However!

As you say, I am likely to have another bike after this horrid war is over. The men don't call it 'horrid' in their songs. A rather more sanguinary adjective is used. I shall, if not in that peculiarly hard and rocky state, of which you complain in your letter, get a bike and sidecar. It's not far from Redditch to Brum.

Since I became a bloated orficer, I have cut one wisdom tooth and am now proceeding with another. How wise the Army must be making some young subalterns. I shall probably be unbearable when I return. By the way I shall begin to agitate for leave in a week or two, then I may have a chance of getting it before the year's out with luck under present conditions.

Things have been very quiet round our part of late, so I have no hair raising experiences to relate. I nearly shot a couple of unfortunate trees the other night under the impression that they were following me.

No, all I had for dinner was lemon squash.

Cheero, girl

Geoff.

8th S.S.R.
27/9/15

Dear Girl,

Just received your alarming letter, & am writing at once to try and put you off, not put you off writing letters, but to try my best to stop you from going in for Science.

If my humble little say has any weight, I beg of you on bendèd knees to go in for medicine. For you to become a science girl would be an absolute catastrophe. Science men are bad enough, but science girls –, Ugh! Horrible! Please don't, for the love of Allah: as Arthur would probably remark, having now become an amateur Asiatic.

Can't say I like the idea of your going to the University at all until "we come back again", then by all means.

I shall be in a perpetual state of anxiety that you might get snapped up by one of those plausible youths, who are snapping everything up, when they ought to be on another job altogether. Only lately I've felt bitter against that kind. Formerly I used to wonder why they were such asses to miss all this holiday and fun. But you see we have had our first officer killed the other night, when I was up, one of the best officers in the regiment. My God! I'd have loved to have had one of the above mentioned swine for just ten minutes, when I saw the stretcher going down! Couldn't feel sorry for the chap, because he finished the sporting way & died without pain, smashed by a trench mortar bomb. I happened to be working on the mining job, in the same trenches where our regiment was. We were strafing the Bosches to glory with a hefty bombardment. I had some poor devils with me who'd only just come out & it was their first spell in the trenches.

Forgive this little hate of mine, but I simply couldn't keep it in.

So my flapper is a thing of the past, is it? And now you consider yourself a full grown woman, at any rate, so it seems from your really novelistic remark about "a woman's privilege". I refuse to guess again about 'Freckles'. My guess suits me down to the ground, & I'll abide by it, woman's privilege or no. And as for the grannie idea, well, we'll leave that till we're in the region of sixty.

By the way I don't know how old you are, are you going to tell me or let your age remain a thing mysterious? I shouldn't do the latter, if I were you or I might in a fit of cynicism jump to the conclusion that you are years older than I, and discontinue writing, which would be disastrous, since writing to blue eyes & – er – red hair is about the most delightful of pastimes I have in this vale of tears (it's raining just now).

This mining is not without its dangers, rather unexpected ones at times. It is rather trying on the nerves, listening for Huns burrowing & expecting them to blow you up at any minute, as witness what happened last night in a shaft where the corporal in charge had the wind up badly.

He was down the shaft going along one of the galleries when suddenly he came upon two Bosches round a corner.

He drew back (all this is his own account) & heard them say (in English) "It's only 10 feet to the bottom of the shaft." So entirely convinced was he that they were wily Bosches that he let fly with his revolver several times, then retired rapidly & reported to the officer at the top, who went down & of course found nothing.

Naturally we are returning this imaginative fellow to his regiment. I have no fancy to be mistaken for a Hun by any fool who has the jumps.

In another case a miner listening in one of the galleries swore he could hear the Germans quite near, talking in one of their galleries. An officer and two men he said. He could tell it was an officer, for in spite of the fact that he couldn't speak German himself, he could easily detect the cultured accent of the officer! These are not '*cum grano salis*' stories, they're facts.

I've written you quite enough boring material for one dose so
　　　Cheero, Edith, girl!
　　　　& best of luck in your MEDICAL CAREER.

8th S. Staffords.
B.E.F.
13/10/15

Dear Edith,

Thanks awfully for the letter & papers, & so glad to hear you're a medical. Science would have been the limit, & the people in it, well – you'll have met them by now, so 'nuff said.

As you say, the medical feminine section will have 'some' girls in it, if you & the charming Miss Gibb are to grace the dreary tiers of lecture halls, & to think that there will only be unappreciative Japs & too-appreciative abominables to sit in the desks behind! I hope you will succeed in being pipped in all exams. For You and Co to pass out, before Ainscow, Boothby Ltd put in a reappearance, would be truly tragic! As it is you'll be beastly superior to we [*sic*] kids, I'm 20 & ten months by the way.

Life lately has been rather exciting for me. No, don't jump to the conclusion that I was in the big push, our regt was miles away. This little adventure was a personal affair only.

I left the R.E. some time ago & went with my trusty miners to the trenches occupied by our Brigade, there to take over the mines. The preceding Brigade handed them over to us as 'all quiet and correct'. Mon dieu! I should smile!

After we'd been there two days an R.E. officer came up & inspected the two saps [*narrow communicating trenches*] I was looking after, then went down those under the charge of the other mining officer. Out of curiosity he went down an old gallery half full of water, & you can imagine his surprise when he came upon an instrument like a magnified telephone receiver stuck in the wall & connected to wires which ran into the darkness ahead of him. He examined & disconnected it & found the word '*unten*' stamped on it, also two more German words. He came back to the open air where we were waiting for him & then we three officers went down & explored the old gallery. Right at the end we found the Germans had run one of their galleries into ours. We found in the German gallery a water pump, which they used to pump water from their own gallery into our old one. Also there was the rest of the telephonic instrument, a beautiful and complicated affair. Being men of average clay & not of the true heroic mould we only explored a few yards of the German gallery, which was full of nasty corners; we only had one rifle between us, which was as good as useless in such cramped quarters.

Well, out we went again leaving the instrument so as not to alarm the wily Bosch, before we had sent for the wherewithal to blow him to —— Glory.

After a short time on top, three of us went down again, intent on bagging the instrument. Myself in the lead as I had an electric torch & rifle, followed by a corporal, the R.E. officer bringing up the rear.

These saps are four foot high by three broad, so you haven't much room for fancy antics, & the one we were in had eighteen inches of water in it. The water made a frantic noise round our legs. Well, we got round a slight bend leading into the straight into which the Bosch gallery came at right angles, when suddenly, as the penny horribles say, "a shot rang out". Only it didn't ring. In the confined space all we got for our money was a spiteful "poop!" from a revolver. Yours truly dropped his torch in the water & got one shot off, while the others "made good their retreat". Once more it didn't take me long to discover the hero profession was off for me. The revolver shooter was entirely concealed round the corner, his weapon only pointing round. A revolver at six yards range going rapid is just a wee bit unhealthy in a 4' x 3' space, so I dropped my rifle & after a Jewish attempt to find my torch, which I'd just bought at the excessive price of £1, I cleared to the next corner, where I found the others. Then the R.E. officer went to the top of the shaft again & had filled sandbags sent down, also explosives, & the corporal & I laid a charge. Took us three hours. This was made rather exciting by the fact that the Huns were almost certainly doing the same thing further along the gallery. We got our blow off first though.

Some sport! What!

Cheero, dearie!

Geoff.

Moustache, I'm sorry to say, refuses to become even red.	8th S. Staffords. B.E.F. 4/11/15

Edith, dear,

What a rotter I am not to have written before! Honestly, I've started twice but have been interrupted, & I can never pick up the threads of a letter once I stop. Fount of inspiration dries up & all that sort of rot, you know.

Those cigarettes & things came most aptly, I was in the trenches & supplies had run out. It was awfully sporting of you to send them, I was frightfully bucked to get 'em. The weapon*, too, will no doubt be useful in my present saps which are only four by two foot six.

---

* ?paperknife? Edith must have sent him something small and sharp.

Sorry the 'abominables' & 'ladies' are so trying. I'd rather like to have the wretched Timmins you mention in my platoon & take him out on patrol. His moustache also might come in useful to keep him warm, for the ogre of winter is at hand & it's very very chilly o' nights.

You would be amused, not shocked, to see my preparations for ensnaring the Goddess of slumber & thwarting the God of Cold. First I put on a great coat & then a burberry. Five sandbags on each foot, a night cap on my golden locks & finally I creep into a postbag which reaches my middle. And even then I'm cold about the toes. Perhaps wearing boots at night does it. As I tie the post bag round, a sudden attack would probably find me tracking it down a communication trench à la sack race with a nasty Bosch encouraging my efforts at the point of a sanguinary bayonet. Rather undignified, what!

I have been leading the gay life. A few days ago I made my way to a certain town near at hand most of the houses of which are still standing & there I went to a pierrot show! Amazing, isn't it?

It's run by young subalterns, who do nothing else & who are admirably assisted by two petite and charming Belgian girls. What a glorious job! For the subs, I mean. It was a ripping show & would not disgrace anything of the kind I've seen in that land which once existed & may still do so for all I know, namely England.

We had a champagne supper after it, about the most gorgeous thing I've had for what seem years. Course after course – till we thought we'd – well – bust. And in such a topsy-turvy order, too. Thinking each course was the last we did ample justice to all. Thank God I wasn't wearing a belt!

You may possibly be pleased to hear I've sent home for the scarf you knitted me last winter, & which I left behind for the summer months.

I saw a Bosch 'plane brought down today. No half measures this time. A 'plane, when hit, usually glides into safety in its own territory. This one fell straight down fluttering & turning like a scrap of paper dropping.

Leave has started! I may get it next February or possibly even before. My pater, however, has gone to Flushing in Cornwall to see whether he can get better there & Mother has gone down there too, to be with him, so I expect I'll spend the greater part of my five days there, though I expect I'll have a flying trip to Brum. In fact, I must, mustn't I? Oh! For a cushy wound & a month or two at home.

My one other correspondent has become engaged, you'll be relieved to hear. I still write, however, she's such a sport. Do I see you frown. Yes, I do. Can't be helped though.

Cheero, darling.

Geoff.

Envelope marked: Not Beech Hurst, Somerset Rd.

Mining Section
51st Inf. Brigade
B.E.F.
27/xi/15

Cheero, Darling,

How are you? I'm in fine form, though in the trenches. Muddy from head to foot & damp at all the joints. Fortune smiles, however, a glowing brazier stands at my feet & I'm in a large, dry dug-out. What more could one want? I've had a mouldy night of it, sinking a shaft under the most trying conditions of wet, cold & bad luck. I'm on what we call 'graveyard shift', midnight till eight in the morning, & during that time am responsible for all the mines. Had two scares, Huns reported working two yards from our gallery, which meant yours truly lying on his tummy in sodden clay for half an hour & hearing nothing. Second scare that the Bosch was breaking into our gallery, so I had to explore with much shaking at the knees, a revolver & no light only to find the asses in our gallery had the wind up & were "seeing things".

During the last week I (please excuse the redundant Ego, but it's one of my chief interests out here) I have had as much excitement as is good for me. Day before yesterday the winged death missed my head by a scant two inches while I was poking a too curious head above the parapet. Rather fortunate it missed, as the stretcher bearers would have had a rotten time taking me down. I'd just waded through two hundred yards of sludge about two foot deep. 'Fraid the language would have been as warm as the place I would have gone to.

Yesterday three crumps [*type of explosive*] made themselves considerably *de trop* by landing within ten yards of our dugout, one smashing the entrance. But we're getting used to such trifling things as shells in this particular part of the world. It's no exaggeration to say that more shells, friendly & otherwise, have passed over our heads during the last fortnight here than during the whole of the time we've been out elsewhere.

But the greatest adventure of all never came off. The powers that be arranged that a party of bombers should attack part of the enemy trenches & we miners should go across with a party of men with 20 lbs of gun cotton apiece & blow up certain strongholds. A lucky event prevented this, however, & as I was one of the officers going over, I'm congratulated on still being alive. It's all in the day's work & a little excitement now & then is warming for the coldest men, to parody a little.

Your suggestion that I should get home with dysintry [*sic*] is really the limit. I know you are confoundedly matter-of-fact in your letters, but really – dysintry – how horribly prosaic. Doesn't your sense of the romantic shudder at the idea? But it evidently doesn't or you wouldn't have written such a shockingly materialistic remark. What would our grandmothers say to the modern girl's letter to her – er – belovéd at the front? *Vide hoc.*

Algernon, my best belovédst,

How is your stomach? I do hope the Carter's little liver pills have removed the yellow shade from your beautiful green eyes. I have just heard of a cure for your – – – (Deleted by Censor.)

I hope you see how prostrated I am from the shock. Please don't let it occur again.

Why are you so disturbed about your golden locks? I should let 'em stay in the flapper formation. Looks ripping enough.

Do please send the socks by all means, there's nothing I need more out here, except – no, I won't tell you the exception, you might become swell-headed or even sentimental, *le dernier cri* in tragedy.

You seem very anxious to look more beautiful than you are pending my arrival on leave. To begin with that were impossible. Also you'd soon give it up, if you could only see the object of these preparations. Blue clay hardened & dried is its chief adornment.

Its auburn locks are matted with earth. One eye is encircled with blue, its moustache shows up for once being tinted with the same predominant colour. No, an officer out here is by no means the debonair and immaculate creature one sees at home in such large quantities.

The luxury of washing is non-existant [*sic*], a week marks the period I last saw soap. So

Cheero, Girl

Geoff.

This is the first letter that we have from Edith, and so may be the first that Geoffrey kept. Christmas was approaching and Edith evidently sent him an assortment of presents, including a loving letter.

Telephone   Beechcroft
Edgbaston 632   1, Beech Lanes
                                                         Birmingham
                                                         11/12/15

My dear one.

There's a simply lovely moon tonight and I'm just in the very mood for watching it so please don't mind if this letter is very daft. I usually wait until I'm in a more sensible mood to write to you but tonight I simply can't. I must write to you now.

I wonder what you are doing just now – just this very moment. I wish I knew that you were watching the moon too but I expect you're far too busy for that. I shall just have to imagine you are, for I'm simply longing for 'un peu d'amour' tonight.

Do tell me what it is you want most out there. I want to know. I'll promise not to get swell-headed or anything like that, but as you see I can't promise not to get sentimental as I've already got it frightfully badly. How can I soften your hard heart and make you tell me? Is there any way? There's something I want too – oh! So badly – but it's a secret. I'm afraid it will be the first secret I ever kept. My wish – so important and mysterious – is known to the gods in Olympia and so is destined to come true.

You see, a few days ago, when the Christmas puddings were being made, I took the opportunity of making my humble appeal. I recited the mystic rite, stirred the pudding and wished. So I still have hope.

There's somebody singing downstairs and the words just fit in with my mood. I wish you could hear them. Do you know what they are?

> "*Night and the stars are gleaming*
> *Tender and true*
> *Dearest my heart is dreaming*
> *Dreaming of you.*"

I hope you aren't feeling very cynical when you read this because you'll say "Fancy dreaming of anyone all covered over with blue earth!" But you know blue ought to suit you because it's supposed to suit me, so it doesn't really matter.

I've taken a frightful dislike to all these very immaculate officers who wander along New Street such a lot. When you and Arthur went away I got the weird idea into my head that all the others ought to have gone too and it annoyed me excessively to see that they hadn't.

By the way Arthur told me to tell you that he's still very bucked with life in a dug-out but he ' 'oped to 'ell it would be over soon'. Dear old Arthur! You see, what annoys him is the fact that he hasn't seen a girl for four months. It's very sad isn't it?

We've had some small photos of him, printed from those large ones that he had taken before he went out and they look simply topping. Were you ever vain enough to have [your photo taken in]* your uniform?

---

* illegible because paper damaged, but reconstructed from the context.

Arthur Ainscow

If so why did you never send me one? I should have been frightfully bucked.

Oh. I was forgetting. I'm awfully sorry I gave you such a very bad shock by mentioning such a thing as d———y. But what am I to do? I don't want you to get wounded & I <u>do</u> want you to come home now because February is such a long, long time away. Can you suggest anything less likely to shock you? I'm afraid I can't write a letter that our grandmothers would consider to be a fit and proper one for a young lady to write to her belovèd. Do you mind very much? I once offered to pretend to be your grandmother, you know, and I'm sure I should have done that awfully well, but you wouldn't let me.

Oh! What a shame! The moon has just gone under a cloud. I wish there were no clouds, do you? I suppose I had better take the hint and finish.

Goodnight, my dear man in khaki.

Edith.

Don't you think this is nice?

The Vagabond

Dunno a heap about the what an' why,
Can't say 's I ever knowed,
Heaven to me's a fair blue stretch of sky,
Earth's jest a dusty road

Dunno the name's o' things or what they are
Can't say's I ever shall.
Dunno about God – He's just the noddin' star
Atop the windy hill.

Dunno about life – it's jest a tramp alone
From wakin' time to doss.
Dunno about Death – it's jest a quiet stone
All over grey wi' moss.

An' why I live, an why the old world spins,
Are things I never knowed;
My mark's the gipsy fires, the lonely inns,
And just the dusty road.

To ye very deare knight of ye
                            faire Ladye Edythe.

These with greetings.

Ye – er– socks were woven by ye own hand of ye aforesaid loved ladye.

Each stitch is linked together by the well wishes and —— (censored) of thy belovèd.

Ye other various and weird contents may perhaps bring ye that complaint of which ye spoke whereby ye may be returned to the longing arms of your own

Edythe

Ye 11th daye of ye 12th month in the yeare of our Lord 1915

Mining Section
51st Inf. Brigade
B.E.F. 21/xii/15

Dear Girl,

What a topping letter that last of yours. No, fortunately I wasn't feeling at all cynical, when I read it, as you feared I might. You must have a curious idea of my character. Cynical! When reading a letter from you! Ye Gods!

"Night & the stars are gleaming." A romantic time enough to write; I read under far different, but no less romantic conditions. Thirty odd feet below the surface of Belgium & somewhat nearer the Huns than the people in the trenches, but the Bosche was many a long mile from my mind at that moment. "Dearest, my heart is dreaming". A ripping song, though to look at the mud plastered scoundrel named "me", you would scarcely imagine he had a heart at all, much less a sentimental one. By the way I heard it the very same night you wrote, & though we mayn't both have been star gazing, no doubt the thoughts were not far different.

So you can see I'm getting sloppy too. It's excusable after a month or two in sandbag land. Arthur is apparently the same.

A million thanks for the present, is it birthday or Xmas? You see it arrived half way between, I was twenty one on the thirteenth. Bow wow!

So now I'm legally a man, & sole controller of my destiny, at least I should be were I not in the Army, thus the above named burden is taken off my feeble shoulders *pro. tem.* Suppose I'll have to start training as a destiny controller as soon as the war's over.

By the way, your parcel had greater adventures than you possibly expected when you despatched it to the unknown. Not least of these was the fact that it was gassed, & me with it. Not the really "frightful" kind, but the milder lacrimose shells. Rummage in the forgotten rooms of your brain & you will remember "lacrimae" means tears: Hence, lacrimose shells = tear shells. Q.E.D.

The abominables dropped six on a road in front of me. I was off the mark in fine style, did three hundred yards in record time & got through the worst of it safely. But it certainly makes you weep. My incomparable ahem – er – Grecian nose had a colour, which would put to shame the proboscis of the most seasoned of port wine squires, & my beautiful hazel; no, blue, no, grey (pause while I fetch a mirror)

Ah! – er– green eyes have never been so blood shot since the time I was so soundly smacked for cutting the cat's whiskers & attaching a tin can to its tail. (I didn't really do these things you know, it's what you call poetic license. I was by nature an angelic child, in those bygone days before I was twenty one.)

It's fortunate that you weren't there (at the gas, not the cat, episode) or, between sneezes, you might have heard most curious words issuing from my ruby lips. Perhaps, however, your innocent ears (er – pearl shell ears) would have taken them for Belgian, so all would have been well.

Besides attaining such perfection as an elocutionist one is apt to become something of a thinker out here. Thinking which shell is going to hit you, you know. In other words we are having quite a lively time.

I envy you your opportunity for wishing, while pudding stirring. There are no puddings to stir out here unfortunately. At least, my belovèd Mater has sent one out, but it has passed the stirring stage & has reached the "For eating, boil for one hour" stage, & then be careful not to swallow the lucky sixpence. By the way, can I wish, if I get that? If so I'll eat the whole pudding.

Failing puddings I thought of inventing "wish-times" to suit my position, viz: (whatever that means) If the next shell hits my dug out, I can wish.

But I'm rather afraid that won't do, as my first wish will be that it hadn't, & I wish to wish something far dearer than that.

But enough of this wishing or I shall soon get so fuddled that I shan't know which wish is the wish I wish to wish.

You must not be enraged if I don't send you a present exactly at Xmas, but short of chopping a Bosche's head off & sending it to you embalmed in dubbin, after the gentle Oriental custom, I can think of nothing else. True, there are a few lace shops not far away, but the nature of the garments displayed in the window is too much for so thin skinned an individual as me.

Well here's my Xmas toast. Health, warmth & happiness to all things British, & crumps, wet dugouts and bad trenches for our friend over the way. To wit, Herr Bosche.

Best wishes for your Xmas party & don't forget the round robin for Arthur and I [*sic*].
– Goodbye, Dear Heart
Geoff.

Beechcroft
Beech Lanes
Birmingham
1 . 1 . 16

Telephone
Edgbaston 632

Dearest,

I've had such a nice lazy day today except of course the very first part of it which was decidedly energetic. I daren't tell you what time it was when I got up or I might get very severely reprimanded! <u>Could</u> you be very severe with me? I can't even imagine it (Botheration! I shall have to be severe with this pen. It's always running dry.) This afternoon I gave myself up to dreams. It's excusable being New Year's day, isn't it? I sat in a big, big arm chair – yes, perhaps there would have been room for two – in front of a red, red fire and though and thought and dreamed and dreamed. Have you ever made fire-pictures? Please don't say you're above such things even although you are twenty-one now. They're awfully sweet. I think you figured as the 'mud-plastered scoundrel', as you call yourself, because you see: unfortunately, the colour of the flames clashed with your hair! Besides I like to think of you as you are now, although if I took on trust your description of yourself, what a picture I should have to be sure. – a mud-plastered scoundrel, with green eyes, Grecian nose and ruby lips. No, I don't like it. I much prefer my own picture. Last night we all went down to Gibb's to bring the New Year in and give him a hearty welcome. The order of the day was to make as much noise as possible. Prompt at twelve o'clock twelve shots were fired (not to remind us that there was a war going on) and the darkest man with a lucky sixpence was brought into the house. Heaps of toasts were drunk but I had two all to myself. You can guess what they were but I'll tell you all the same. They were to you and Arthur. Good Luck. I wonder what you were both doing just at that very minute. I hope the New Year wasn't started in the way we intend to go on because really it would be very shocking indeed if it was. We all started kissing one another all the way round!! It didn't matter who they were, whether you knew them or not before, you kissed them all the same. Terrible isn't it? I got in such a muddle over this proceeding. Instead of wishing people a Happy New Year I started saying 'Goodbye'. Not that I always kiss everybody when I say goodbye you know!

It was most awfully nice of you to think of sending me a present at Xmas but of course there's only one thing I really want and as my 'wish' for that has already gone up to Heaven I'm not worrying any further. Oh, but I forgot, there is something I want. May I ask? Please can you pretend you've lost one of your badges and send it to me? – mud of Flanders and all. I'm sure it would be frightfully easy to lose one artistically out there and as you must have been a model of righteousness to your men in that respect up till now, they won't notice very much if you transgress for once. Please do. Of course, if it's going to be a very serious

disadvantage to you I can easily send you a safety-pin to replace it!!!
(Tut-tut, that's very wicked isn't it?) It isn't really like a button though, is
it? But 'nough said. If I beg you not to be too annoyed with me you will
think I have a still curiouser idea of your character, won't you?

You'll be very amused when I tell you that I wore a veil the other
night – to protect my – er – beauty from the stormy elements. I think
it's the second time I've ever worn one so you see I'm coming on. I felt
exactly like a caged lion and it's the greatest wonder that I hadn't eaten
my way through to the outer air before I reached my destination. Of
course one rude person told me how very 'fetching' I looked with a veil
on but I expected that and put it down to jealousy. It sounds just like
one of Arthur's sayings, doesn't it? Have you ever had any experience of
them? One of his favourite compliments to me was: 'Edith, you'd be
awfully good looking if it wasn't for your face!! Of course I used to reply
by telling him what a remarkable ressemblance [*sic*] there was supposed
to be between us! The first time I wore a veil was when I came down to
Camberley. That was why the car nearly gave up the ghost that weekend.
Father laughed all the way down there, except when he was talking nicely
to the engine.

I had a little private note from Arthur the other day in which he
entrusted me with a secret which he kept for about two months. He's
been slightly wounded and now is able to display the honourable scars
of war. It was on the knee where he was hit by a shrapnel bullet. I
suppose you've heard that they've evacuated Suvla Bay where he was at
the Dardanelles so we don't know where he is now.

By the way please don't be too superior to me now you are twenty-
one, will you? I'm not so very, very much younger than you, you know.
I have a birthday coming along very soon now, on the 9th of this month
to be exact. So I'm not <u>much</u> behind you. I'm going to be eighteen then.
If you don't get the lucky sixpence on Christmas day you can have your
'wish' on the ninth. Make it an extra-specially nice one, 'cause it's my
birthday.

I'm glad you were such an angelic child but I'm afraid I can't say that
I was. I'm always getting the misdeeds of my early youth related to me at
the most awkward moments. Still, you must remember, you always grow

up the opposite of what you were when you were a child!

Well, Good-night, dear. I wish you hadn't grow'd up and become a 'controller of destinies', because then I could sing:

> "*Sleep, thou darlingest boy of mine,*
> *I will rock thee, my child,*
> *And guard thee.*"

But I forgot, it's you who are guarding us isn't it. So Goodnight once more.

Yours,

Edith

P. S. Are you coming to the panto with me again this year? February's long a'coming.

Mining Section
51st Inf Brigade
B.E.F.

Edith, Girl,

Happiest of New Years, though I hope you won't be so rash as to pass any exams till the war's over for reasons given heretofore.

I come home on leave from the 3rd to the 11th Jan. Will you been [*sic*] near Falmouth or London during that time, 'cause I'm afraid all my leave will be spent in the South of England owing to my Pater being there, you know.

Ye Gods! I wish we were still in Brum so that I could see all my friends and relations, and – er – other friend. Still I'll have to hope you'll be down south.

What does the C. in my name stand for? Christopher, Clarence, Claude, Cuthbert? No, nothing so swanky. It's Charles! Ahem! What! What! Chase me!

I should have loved to have been there, when you were drying your hair before the fire and wearing that *très chic* blue frock. We might have played that horrid game of Postman's Knock. Just à deux. What?

I have to go up to the trenches tonight to get my pass. Isn't it awful. I might get hit. True I've escaped for seven months, but then tonight's the night. At 5.30 a.m. tomorrow I leave for home. Still I must perforce be brave & go up once more (I'm in rest camp now.) Not till this evening have I realised what a terrible place the firing line is. I might be shot or shelled or gassed or bombed. I may fall into a deserted trench & be left to drown. What if they blow a mine? What if aeroplanes start dropping hate? What if – but why continue, I could write a volume of "what ifs". And even should I escape all these my nerves are sure to give way under the strain. I'll have to pray or get drunk or something to steady them or numb them. Heigho! What a life! I see the Irony of Fate stalking me even now in these comfortable billets, well, I hope she falls into a shell hole on the way up.

You want a nickname for me? Call me anything you like, but do try and avoid the pit which the obvious presents.

My hair is carroty, ginger anything you like, but then that is the obvious. I ceased to worry about those nicknames at the age of 10.

Yours, dear Girl.

Geoff.

Smile awhile for while you smile another smiles and soon there's miles & miles of smiles and life's worth while because you smile.

[written by Edith in pencil on the back of the last page of Geoffrey's letter]

77 Tunnelling Coy.

<u>N.B.</u> ⟶ R.E. B.E.F.

22/1/16

Dear Girl,

I have just received your letter, which has been much delayed at various spots in this benighted country.

Explanation as under.

My battalion has gone back to rest for a month about thirty miles behind the line. I am transferring to the Engineers, if I can possibly manage it & so have been left behind with the above Company pending results. Your treasured epistle arrived here (in the RE. Rest camp) while I was *aux tranchées* & they didn't trouble to send it up. At the same time I got the round robin. Please either thank or give my love to the merry company, who appended their names. Use your discretion. Any way [*sic*] I was awfully bucked to get it & appreciate the happy thought of the senders.

Now I have a confession to make, which gives me more pain than any crump could, since it will probably put an end to what has hitherto been the most delightful correspondence *de ma vie*.

I've been on leave without making any effort to see you. Very blunt, but I had to get it over. That's why this correspondence will be broken off. You'll never forgive me. My only excuse you may consider cowardly, since I take shelter behind an invalid & a lady's skirts. My people were at Falmouth, which is just about the furthest point in England from anywhere. Only a handful of miles from Land's End. As I spent two of my precious seven days in getting there and back there wasn't much left for a tour to Brum. I was two nights in London with the Mater & my cousin, the dark boy, you possibly remember.

So I may have received the last letter you'll ever write me, though this isn't the last you'll get from me. I never give up a thing I want badly without some sort of struggle. But I think I've said enough for the present. You've possible [*sic*] torn up these pages already, so why should I continue with a recitation of my very mediocre adventures?

At best it would be anticlimax of the most flagrant type.

Geoff.

Alice Boothby, Geoffrey's mother.

Telephone
Edgbaston 632,

Beechcroft
Beech Lanes,
Birmingham.
23.1.16

Geoff, dear,

I was bucked to death to hear that you were coming home on leave but why ever didn't you put the other way round? You ought to have told me first that you couldn't get up to B'ham and <u>then</u> that you had got leave. It would have saved me quite a lot. You see, as it was, I was first raised to the heights of bliss and then plunged into the depths of despair, kind of style!! Still I had guessed ages ago that you wouldn't be able to reach this out-of-the-way region unless you suddenly developed a pair of wings or joined the Flying Corps, so it wasn't <u>quite</u> as bad as it sounds. I'm longing to hear what sort of a time you had. How are your mother and father? I hope you made it quite clear to them that they've got to hurry up and be quite well and up in Brum by your next leave!

I'm feeling the effects just now. I've been reading 'Omar Khayyam', and 'A Way of Life' by William Osler. It's truly wonderful and perhaps you may not believe it but I feel <u>almost</u> good. That's why I'm writing to you – just to see if it won't have some effect. I've had a spasm of 'Omarism' just lately, but the other one is a more curious taste. In case you didn't know, it's a lecture to the Yale students and I don't agree with it a scrap. Still, it does make you feel good and that's one thing accomplished.

I'm trying to write this by the light of the fire – "Dusk and the shadows falling". – It's a shame to shut out the dusk and I can't see any longer so just wait for a wee while.

Dusk has fallen so I can proceed.

No! I wouldn't be so rash as to pass any exams this year. Witness my terminal results which I haven't the courage to tell you. Also we had a metals exam the other day. Personally I don't see why I need to know anything about any metals except Gold, silver and Copper but they evidently seem to expect you to. I went to the exam just for a bit of fun (I'm afraid I've got a curious sense of humour) and got frightfully bored with playing noughts and crosses and other interesting games by myself. My hair came down in the middle though and provided amusement for myself and others.

The man informs us that he's going to take a fortnight's holiday before he marks the papers to guard against nervous shock !

I'm afraid you would never recover if you saw some of the specimens we have at the University. We have acquired a few more – er – men this term. Two of them are absolutely bald and I'm sure they can't be less than sixty! Most exciting sort of individuals! Still we ought not to grumble. We've got one real live 'occifer'. Just think of it. Water in the desert isn't to be compared with it.

I've decided what I'm going to do in the very, very distant future when I'm through. I shall have a dog, a cat, a very talkative parrot and a young pale-blue motor. Then I shall find the sweetest house that ever was and live in it. I expect you'll say that the cat will eat the parrot, the dog will eat the cat and I shall die of melancholia but all the same that's what I'm going to do.

It's a good job you weren't here when I was drying my hair by the fire isn't it? I wonder if we should have been bored then?

I wish your leave had been longer.

Well,

        Cheero, Geoff.

          Yours.

            Edith

Telephone
Edgbaston 632

        Beechcroft
        1, Beech Lanes
        Birmingham
        26/1/16

Geoff dearest

I hardly know what to say to you. Surely you knew that I would understand why you couldn't come up to see me during your seven days. Of course I had hoped you would be able to come because I couldn't help it, but all the time I knew it was practically impossible. You see I know what it would be like if Arthur were to come home.

I wrote to you the other night and I tried to make you think I didn't mind <u>very</u> much, but I did – awfully. I had to go up north too that week and you seemed farther away than ever.

You silly boy! Did you really think I would stop writing to you? Sometimes I wonder if my letters bore you very much. I should simply hate to think that and you would tell me if they did, wouldn't you?

If you only knew — but you don't so it doesn't matter. I'm a girl and I can't help wondering all sorts of silly things. The chief among them is whether I do bore you very badly. You see, it's a year now since you've seen me, isn't it? Anyway I'm comforted by the assurance that you do want my letters very badly.

Please tell me all about what you did when you were home.

> Yours,
>
> Edith.

P.S. This is how I felt when I got your letter

Nothing to do but work
Nothing alas! Alack!
Nowhere to go but out
Nowhere to come but back.
Nothing to breathe but air
Nothing to sing but song
Nowhere to fall but off
Nowhere to stand but on.

Nothing to weep but tears
Nothing to comb but hair
Nothing but sights to see
Nothing but clothes to wear

Nothing to eat but food
Nothing to quench but thirst
Nothing to have but what we've got
Thus thro' life are we cursed.

R.E.
B.E.F.
3/2/16

Edith, Dearest,

My relief on getting your letters is hardly describable. I wanted to burst for joy, to fire my revolver rapidly, to yell in the mines, to go out and slay half a dozen Huns. In fact I experienced the most perfect joie de vivre imaginable.

But I'm a stolid sort of individual, so – though only with the greatest difficulty – I managed to restrain myself & limit myself to the usual inane grin, which I adopt when reading your letters, thereby betokening complete happiness.

You dear girl! I can't think why you imagined your letters bored me. I really did try my utmost in my last letter to show you what they are to me. But I'm afraid my pen must be very inexpert to have let such an idea ever occur to you.

I've made two attempts to write to you from the trenches, whence I have come this very evening, but I was interrupted both times. The first was a wire to go & listen to suspected mining noises, & the second was to tie up a wounded officer, who was brought into my dug-out. Fortunately he wasn't seriously smashed, though he bled like Old Harry. I tried to console him by telling him he'd be in England in no time, but, would you believe it, he didn't want to go back, as it was only his second experience of trenches. Some people don't know when they're on a good thing.

The poems in your last were delightful, I learnt the "Vagabond" by heart. Ah! Do I see you smile a cynical smile? You think I said that to please you. I deny the charge. In peace times I used to read more than the average child.

Sorry to hear Arthur's wound was capable of bringing him home. Isn't it about time he had leave, or don't they get any in the Medit. E.F.? By the way, you never sent me his address.

Have you got any small good photos of your belovèd self? If so would it be too much trouble to send one right away now, before you forget? I've just sent home for one of mine, which I'll send on to you in case you would like one.

You ask me what I did on leave. Well only two things stand out. I didn't speak to one pretty girl, or ugly one for that matter, & I went to "Tonight's the Night" & saw [*George*] Grossmith for the first time. Have you seen him? He's top-hole. We have all the songs from the above on our gramophone out here, or rather I should say gramophones, as we have one in rest camp and one in trenches. You see we have an absolutely crumpproof dug-out now, so we can luxuriate. Also our chances of being pipped are just about halved, & nervous strain is quite a thing of the past.

Your description of how you're going to live when you're through is all very well, but I think I could improve upon it.

Au rev. Darling,

Geoff.

B.E.F.
19/2/16

Dearest,

Is it by chance or design that your letters of late have arrived, bearing with them a faint perfume? Because it's there alright & its simply ripping! The letter seems more intimate than ever somehow. I couldn't detect it in the last possibly because I'm victimised by a cold in the head & a cough in the throat complicated by several lesser ailments. My iron constitution, however, fortified with couple of the M.O.'s [*Medical Officer*] celebrated No. 9 pills, has weathered these inroads & I'm fast returning to the land of the living, not to say lively.

Have you heard of the No. 9 pill? The M.O. doles it out for coughs, colds, toothache, slight wounds, tetanus, typhoid and frost-bite. Also I shouldn't be surprised if it turned out to the much-sought Elexir [*sic*] of Life!

Anyway, allow me to recommend it to your father as a work saver, if nothing else.

Arthur seems to have had rather a rough passage. Thank God he's come through with nothing worse than magnified feet! It makes me feel ashamed of the way we carry on war in this part of the world. Riding up to the trenches in motors, buying all the latest magazines on the way & living in crump-proof dugouts, where we are surrounded by undreamed of luxuries, gramophones, beautiful, through rather risqué pictures, & all sorts of comforts.

But even we cannot always escape the shelling, which, as you say, is a mere detail, provided of course, they don't make too close an acquaintance with you, there I'm rather afraid you're the mere detail. I'm east of Ypres & the papers may tell you of the little jokes the Hun will persist in playing us there. Decidedly he has his tail up now-a-days. Unfortunately we're so thoughtless as to have ours up too, which makes the times slightly less boring than of old.

Need you have asked whether I would have liked to be with you, all alone in that cosy chair with the countless cushions? You scarcely realise, it's evident, how you tantalise me with such pictures, which you are constantly painting in your letters. For God's sake don't discontinue them, I'm collecting quite a select little gallery for use on wishing times & dream days. I wonder how long it'll be before they'll all jump out of their frames and suddenly become true, real live facts. Time whirls along at a breakneck pace now-a-days, so I'll be an optimist & drive it faster still & risk the broken neck.

I don't care tuppence whether the University puts me down as Dental or Medical, I don't suppose I'll take up either again, it would be such an age before I could qualify.

Can you suggest anything short of staying in the Army on nothing a year? But don't think too long about such boring matters, I want your letter to come rushing along as fast as it possibly can, so

Good Bye, Dear Heart,

Geoff.

Telephone
Edgbaston 632

Beechcroft
1, Beech Lanes
Birmingham
27 . 2 . 16

Geoff, dearest

Your letters bring you so close to me and I only wish they came every other day. That would be far too much happiness to expect though. I'm so sorry. I really didn't mean to tantalise you with the pictures I'm always drawing in my letters. But you must realize that it's also a case of self-torture. You see the one thing necessary to complete the picture is always missing. I won't tell you what that is. If you think <u>very</u> hard, perhaps you may guess. Still I do so love imagining such things and thank you very much for not forbidding them.

I had such a spasm of joy on hearing that fighting is in a more comfortable job now. But the risqué sketches that adorn the walls of your dugout! – Tut tut – I shall have to come and censor them. Such things are not good for your moral welfare. I was allowed the privilege of inspecting my honourable brother's art gallery in his hut at Bovington in the summer but the privilege didn't extent as far as being allowed to censor them. They were truly killing but I won't give him away entirely.

He sent us a lot of snapshots the other day and we were frightfully bucked. I prophesied ages ago that as soon as he got to Egypt he would have his photo taken perched on top of a camel. I'm enclosing one of the snaps for your benefit. Personally I think it's an insult to both of you, don't you? I'm sorry to have to report that he's accumulating a frightful amount of swank! It's very sad isn't it but not altogether unexpected. He's acting Captain of his company and doesn't let us forget the fact. He talks about 'my subs' as though they were the dirt under his feet. It's decidedly funny. You will notice the conspicuous absence of – er – moustache. I suppose that's because of the heat! He had five days leave not long ago to go and see the pyramids so I suppose we shall have a picture of him sitting astride one of them before long. I'm dreading lest on his regal pay – 16/– a day – he'll get hold of a harem and bring it home with him!

I'm so glad you aren't in Egypt!!!

I was going to be so very grandmotherly and tell you how to prevent colds and coughs etc. by changing your boots every time you get your feet wet and by drinking blackberry tea and all sorts of nice things that would beat No. 9 pills into fits. Unfortunately I forgot to put my precepts into practice and I've got that very unromantic ailment myself now. I think you must have put some of the young germs in your last letter just to prevent me being grandmotherly. I think perhaps you had better send me some of your Elixir of life although it doesn't sound half so nice as blackberry tea. I'll send you some socks that I've just finished in exchange. In desperation I nearly knitted the toe of one of them in pink wool but fortunately I eventually got some khaki to match the rest. You would have been annoyed to find one foot pink wouldn't you?

I've thought and thought and thought but I haven't decided yet what you have to go in for. When I was wee and good I used to inform people alternately that I was going to be a lady or a missionary. You couldn't very well be either of those could you!? You see I had a great longing to travel and I thought that to be a missionary was the best way of doing it. I have a vague sort of idea that you are a very travelled person. Are you? Anyway don't stay in the army although you would have a topping time even on £0 a year. Have you counted up all your talents? Do you sing, play, dance, act, paint or write books? Anyway, what matters money? You should say

"*The desert were a paradise*
If thou wert there, if thou wert there". –

–talking to the cat of course!

My photos are really quite good – not bad anyway. Have you changed your mind about wanting one yet?

I shall probably be up in London just before Easter. Coming?

Good bye, my dear one

Edith

P.S. The chair with the countless cushions is still waiting. I'm certain it won't have to wait <u>very</u> long.

Telephone
Edgbaston 632

Beechcroft
1, Beech Lanes
Birmingham
27. 2 . 16

Geoff, dear,

I expect you are wondering why this thusness. But I quite forgot to put this young photo in my other letter. It would really have been a miracle if I had remembered about it because I'm sure you must have noticed what a common weakness it is for people to talk profusely about things they imagine they have enclosed in their letters.

I'm no exception to the general rule.

We have been 'some' walk this morning in the snow just be [*sic*] way of trying to cure my cold! It was ripping although we looked like 'three shies a penny' snowmen when we got back.

If I write too long a letter I shall forget to put the photo in this one too, so

Good-bye, dearest.

Edith

Field Service Postcard

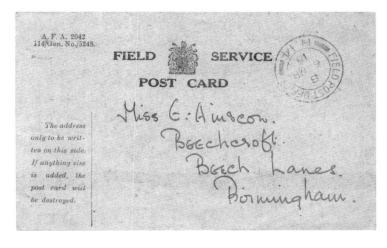

NOTHING is to be written on this side except the date and signature of the sender. Sentences not required may be erased. If anything else is added the post card will be destroyed.

I am quite well.

~~I have been admitted into hospital~~
{ ~~sick~~ } ~~and am going on well.~~
{ ~~wounded~~ } ~~and hope to be discharged soon.~~

~~I am being sent down to the base.~~

I have received your { letter dated 27ᵗʰ Feb
{ ~~telegram,~~ ___
{ ~~parcel~~ ,, ___

Letter follows at first opportunity.

~~I have received no letter from you~~
{ ~~lately.~~
{ ~~for a long time.~~

Signature } C. G. Boothby. 2Lᵗ.
only. }

Date 5 | 3 | 16 .

[Postage must be prepaid on any letter or post card addressed to the sender of this card.]

(25540) Wt.W3497-293 1,130m. 6/15 M.R.Co.,Ltd.

B.E.F. 8/3/16

Dearest,

I'm most sorrowful to tell you that I shan't possibly be able to meet you in town before Easter. Fraid it'll be rather nearer your summer trip to London, when I next come back. All leave has been stopped indefinitely, rumour has it that it doesn't start till the end of June, as was the case last year. If this is so, my seven days of exstatic [*sic*] oblivion will not be due till August. Let's hope & wish, on every possible wishing occasion, that some rotten pessimist has invented this horrid tale out of his own putrid brain.

B.E.F.   8/3/16.

Dearest,
                I'm most sorrowful to tell
you that I shan't possibly be able to meet
you in town before Easter. 'Fraid it'll be
rather nearer your summer trip to London,
when I next come back. All leave has been
stopped indefinitely, rumour has it that it
doesn't start till the end of June, as was
the case last year. If this is so, my
seven days of ecstatic oblivion will not be
due till August. Let's hope & wish, on
every possible wishing occasion, that some
rotten pessimist has invented this horrid
tale out of his own putrid brain.
                I was very unhappy to think that I
might have been possibly the cause of your
unromantic ailment, Grandmother, dear. Do,
please, write & tell me that cold germs won't
go through the post, Miss Medico, just by
way of reassurance. Anyway, if they
do, I've been punished. My cold came on
again, this time accompanied by coughs &
stiffnesses & all sorts of nasty things. In

I was very unhappy to think that I might have been possibly the cause of your unromantic ailment, Grandmother, dear. Do, please, write & tell me that cold germs won't go through the post, Miss Medico, just by way of reassurance. Anyway, if they do, I've been punished. My cold came on again, this time accompanied by coughs & stiffnesses & all sorts of nasty things. In fact, these enemies so pushed the assault, that I had 'to retire ingloriously to bed on coming down from trenches. Disgraceful, what! A soldier, who thinks himself such a brave fellow, driven to bed by a rotten old cold! Hence, by the way, my reason for not writing before, I simply can't write anything worth reading, when I'm physically fed up. Also I really don't think I could write a readable letter every other day, darling. Of course, I could circumnavigate (good word, that!) the difficulty by sending field post cards, but even those impassioned epistles are apt to pale in time, don't you think?

Another Zep. Raid! We expect to find you all living in bomb-proof dugouts, when we come home. We're having a good bit of raiding round us now-a-days, with the difference that the planes come over in broad daylight. Once they had the cheek to give three performances in one day. Rather bad form this hitting below the belt; when we come back to rest camp we expect to rest, & not to have to stop reading or writing or playing to hear them turning up the subsoil in the neighbouring fields. Still I suppose the farmers don't mind much, so we'll (literally) let Herr Airman-Bosch have his fling and sow his wild oats.

I had quite an interesting experience some days ago. At least it would have been interesting, if I hadn't had a temperature & it hadn't been snowing. I had to go up to the French trenches on duty. As it was, my out-look was rather jaundiced. The men (& some of the officers too) had a most unpleasant smell attached to them, which I've never struck on our men (or officers), but then of course, I may have become insensitive to our own particular odour. The only other point that struck me was the enormous quantity of bowing, kow-towing & handshaking in vogue. I started off quite well with a salute & a handshake with the Corps General, but by the time I got to the trench I was so unbalanced that I hardly knew whether to greet the private soldier by licking his boots or falling on his neck, smell & all. However, by exerting my last ounce of self control I managed to refrain from doing either of these things, & merely contented myself with saluting a lance corporal. Persistent and truly insular English speaking carried me through & they had to do all the foreign language talking.

Before I forget let me thank you most awfully for the papers & agologise [*sic*] for not having done so before. Thanks also in anticipation for the socks, which so narrowly escaped growing pink toes. And, again in anticipation, for those photos, which must come rushing along as soon as possible. Mine hasn't come out from home yet, so you mustn't be as impatient as I, dearest.

Personally I think the one of Arthur is more like me than him, but of course I'm no judge. The absence of moustache is an insult to both. Don't ask him, but perhaps he's shaved his off. However, people that live in glass houses — , my photo is just as bad, but then it was taken more than a year ago, surely a year must make some difference to a sub's moustache. We can't be boys for ever. (This is a fit of twenty-one-ness).

My R. E. [*Royal Engineers*] transfer is not yet through but I have hopes that it's on the last lap. The red-tape channels are as numerous as Venetian canals & as intricate as those of Holland (Took me five minutes to think that out.)

Your advice regarding my future didn't help much, but I've given up troubling pro. tem. & so can repeat with sincerity "The trenches were a paradise—" speaking at but not to the cat. Though, of course, the quotation is quite untrue, for if I chanced to find you there I should imagine they were hell on earth and the nerve strain would be terrific till I could get you to safety. The afore-told dugout would be no use, the pictures, you know — .

Good bye, Dear Heart
& buck up & send along another letter for me to grin over & dream about.

Yr.
Geoff.

R.E. B.E.F. 20/3/16

Dearest Girl,

I'm feeling awfully bucked tonight. My transfer's through at last & I'm a real R.E. I have been posted to the company I've been with for the last five months, so my address will [be] the same – minus 8th S. Staff. attached. Did I tell you my pay is now as regal as Arthur's, i.e. sixteen bob a day. I feel a fearful knut,* Royal Engineers, eh what! Think I must start a monocle, but perhaps it would be rather awkward in the mines, so I won't. As it is I'm allowed to wear riding boots & spurs, but I think this rather risky. Last time I wore spurs on horse-back the horse bolted with me. Given 'em up since.

Also at last they've done a photo for me. They say it doesn't flatter me, but I think it does extremely. The moustache is – er – of course rather poor, but the photo was taken when I saw you last, & it's has [*sic*] a chance to come on a bit since then, though the colour's just the same. It didn't go ginger like Arthur's. Suppose the last remark is a case of sour grapes.

Leave has been started again, so I'll be in England sometime about the end of April, D. V. [*Deo volente*] I wonder if we'll see one another this time? My people are still at Falmouth, so we won't build on it this time, it won't be so disappointing. But we are having bad luck, aren't we? It's now a year & two months practically, since we saw one another last. I wonder what we'll think of each other when Giant Circumstance allows us to meet again, – at least I wonder what you'll think of me, I know perfectly well the vice versa part. I do hope you haven't grown much & will look down from six feet on poor little five foot seven and a half with his boots on. i.e. me.

Your photo must buck up & arrive now, there's no excuse. I will send you the R.E. badges as soon as I can get some. You asked for a Staffs badge & I most unforgivable [*sic*] forgot.

The Guards are now in our trench sector. Gad! They're a fine lot of men. All over six feet.

* Jocular spelling of 'nut' = 'dandy', 1911. *O.E.D.*

Their officers are smaller & quite good fellows when you can get them to forget they're Guards & son of lords or better. We have several of them attached to us.

Nearly all my friends in the Staffords have been killed in the fighting round Ypres a few weeks ago. It's a horribly sad thing how many friendships have been made & broken by this war. But it does make one feel really proud to be an Englishman, when one knows how unselfishly one's friends go west. However, the subject will depress you.

Have you heard from Arthur about his visit to the Pyramids? I guess Shepheard's will impress him more. Did I tell you I'd been abroad some myself. Africa, Switzerland, America, Australia, Canada, Teneriffe, Honolulu, & the Southern Seas. You asked me whether I had, but I forget whether I answered the question.

Well, I'm going to bed. Hope I'll dream of our joint interest in our fathomless chair.

Yrs.

Geoff.

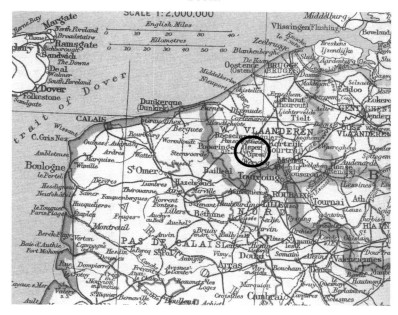

Map showing location of Ypres [Ieper] in Flanders

Telephone   Beechcroft
Edgbaston 632   1, Beech Lanes
                                                                Birmingham
                                              [*undated and no postmark*]

Dearest One,

I must start off by telling you the why and the wherefore of the
pencil and the general wobbliness. You see I'm pretending to be ill just
so that I can miss terminals which begin next week. The powers that be
decided this morning that another week in bed was necessary to put an
end to my – er – miseries so in desperation I decided that the only thing
to do was to write a young [*sic*] note just to inform you that I'm frantically
worried about you, dearest. You men never do take any care of yourselves
(I know such a great lot about it, don't I!!?)

Anyway, do write soon and tell me you're absolutely better.

It's a case of 'imitation is the sincerest form of flattery', isn't it?

I'm truly repentent [*sic*] that the photo is so huge but you see I didn't
know that you wanted one when I had it taken. It looks as if it needs a
piano and a blue silk lamp-shade in your dug-out to go with it.

The umpire says that time's up and it's about time too. My writing is
getting illegible. Still remember the difficulties I'm labouring under.

Good bye darling

                Yrs.

                  Edith

P.S. To ease your mind I haven't got flu. It's something daft wrong
with my neck*

---

*Once, while a medical student, Edith contracted rheumatic fever. It is not clear
whether this was that episode.

R.E. B.E.F. 23/3/16

Dearest,

I've just got your photo. Really I can hardly trust myself to tell you what I thought of it. It's wonderful, you look an absolute darling. It made me almost burst for joy, the most curious and delightful sensation I've ever experienced. In fact the feeling I get, when your letters come along, only magnified ten times. The inane grin of mine was positively face splitting. I had to go straight out for a five mile walk to cool down, but it wasn't much good, I keep slinking out of the mess to my bunk to have just another look at my treasure.

Possibly you think I'm mad – if so please God may I remain mad for the rest of my days, it's the most glorious sensation imaginable.

You must remember I've never seen you with your hair up. Were improvement possible, there it is.

I do wish I hadn't sent that wretched thing of mine, it really doesn't look a bit like me. I don't look quite such an "amateur hero" kind of person. However, I'll have a decent one done when next leave comes along.

How's your terminal illness getting on? I do hope the Easter Vac. has cured it alright. Are you going anywhere for Easter? Oh yes! London, of course.

Gad! Those dreams of yours very nearly did come out of their frames, the nearest approach so far. They've assumed new colour & significance. It's almost a torture to think of that arm-chair.

I must rush off & have another peep.

Your
Geoff.

Edith Ainscow

Telephone
Edgbaston 632

Beechcroft
1, Beech Lanes
Birmingham
29. 3 . 16

Geoff, Dearest,

I've got your photo in front of me just now and I can hardly take my eyes off it even to write to you. I didn't know anything could make anybody so happy. I'm afraid I can't describe to you what I think about it. You'll just have to imagine it. I'm certain you'll be able to. I've been doing nothing but think and dream dreams about it ever since I got it. I've had plenty of time, too, because I had to stay in bed again yesterday and I had your photo just where I could see it.

You would laugh if you could see me now. I've got my head tied up in a sling and I look remarkably like a nun. I suggested that to someone this morning but I was informed that I might <u>look</u> like one but that was quite as far as the resemblance went. I felt very insulted. Still I really think I should make a very nice nun, don't you? Don't you think I might take it up as a profession when I get tired of medicine? I have an invitation to pay a visit to a monastery but I've never had the courage to accept it yet. Not that I'm afraid they might keep me there, you know!! My terminal illness is nearly better now. Holidays have a wonderful effect, don't they? I had the glands amputated or lanced or whatever you like to call it. Thus the thusness.

I'm awfully pleased that you've got your transfer into the R.E.'s. It sounds frightfully swanky. Isn't it supposed to be rather difficult to get an R.E. commission? I always imagined so. By the way how is your dark cousin getting on. He was trying for one, wasn't he?

Arthur has started on his travels again. He's like the proverbial wandering Jew, isn't he? I think he's in Mesopotamia now although it's nearly a month now since we heard that he was starting out in that direction. They have a frantically bad habit of keeping back letters from that quarter of the globe. So you see we haven't heard about his adventures in Cairo, although he sent us a whole heap of photos of himself on a camel with the pyramids and sphinx in the background. It certainly

C. Geoffrey Boothby

looked most incongruous – such a very modern British officer together with such antiquity.

He says that all the fortune-tellers say that he will be home this year. I hope the Egyptian wizards have some special wisdom and foreknowledge that the English ones don't possess.

I didn't know that you were such a very be-travelled person. I only wish I had seen half the places that you have. I don't care for Canada and America. It's the antique places I'm very keen on. I look up to you with awe when I think of all the places you've been to. I try to sound like it but I'm afraid it's rather difficult. I hope you're proud of being such an awe-inspiring person.

Dearest, I wonder when Giant Circumstance will allow us to meet again. I'm a little more satisfied now that I have your photo but only a little. My imagination wanders even more often than before in the realms of fancy and romance.

But please don't let us wonder what we shall think of one another when we do meet. That sometimes rather frightens me. Besides "sufficient for the day is the goodness thereof", isn't it?

Your 'madness' gives me the most wonderful sensation of happiness. I hope that it is absolutely immortal.

Good-night, dear one. I still have to say good-night to my photo.

Yrs.

Edith

Telephone   Beechcroft
Edgbaston 632   1, Beech Lanes
                                                                          Birmingham
                                                                          31 . 3 . 16

Dearest,

At long last I've managed to send you the socks. Still, better late than never. I suppose before long you'll be wanting beauteous silk things in Liberty shades, won't you? Perhaps you don't revel in such vanities though in the trenches, even in the summer.

I nearly got whirled off the face of the earth this afternoon. It was most exciting. I was in the car and a huge ugly motor lorry nearly crashed into us. Annoying in the extreme, wasn't it?

It's the first of April tomorrow – April Fool's day. I wonder, dearest, if we shall see one another before the end of the month. I'm allowed to hope, am not I? I think I would rather pay the penalty if it has to end in disappointment.

<u>Edith.</u>

R.E.B.E.F. 1/4/16

Dearest,

Please excuse paper, but I'm in trenches & haven't got any decent paper.

None of your letters have come along for ages, not since the photo one, in fact. I do hope your attack of terminalitis hasn't become serious. Perhaps the sight of my photo has affected it. But the probable reason is that the people in rest camp are too lazy to send our letters up, & so I expect to find one of the well known envelopes in my pigeon-hole, when I go down tonight.

Jove! It's a gorgeous day. I'm sitting writing in a secluded bit of trench in the most glorious sunshine imaginable. But – & there is often a 'but' out here – the sun brings out other things besides me. The air is humming like a bee-hive. Aeroplanes. The nice weather brings them out to take photographs of the Bosch lines & incidentally ours, also, minutely, of me. But that's not what I object to.

It's all very pretty to see them come sailing up the Eyes of the Army & all that kind of thing, but no sooner are they over our heads than the Bosch takes a very natural dislike to them, & goes as far as to back his annoyance with a few antiaircraft shells.

And this is where the 'but' comes in. The planes don't mind the shells as they're usually miles wide, 'but' we do. The sky first becomes pock-marked with dozens of pretty little white shell-burst & then another hum is added to their general buzz, to wit falling shrapnel crescendo. So I have to hastily diminuendo, in other words go lower & lower into the earth to my wonder dug-out. Just at the moment, however, it's quite alright. The hum continues, the 'planes are still up, & the "Archies" are still busy with their usual futile activity, but it's all over someone else's head at the moment, which is excellent.

Other people's troubles don't interest us at all round here.

I had a most amusing experience the other night. Got arrested by our own men in a bombing post outside the line.

Quite like a penny dreadful. "Hands up!" while they collared my automatic. Then ushered into the bombing post literally at the point of the bayonet. Every one was so excited that we forgot all about the Hun, who was only ninety yards away, so when a "Verey-light" (which is a sort of rocket & beats an arc-lamp into fits for illumination) went up, we didn't trouble to drop flat or stand perfectly still, the only safe course, but continued gesticulations & explanations in loud voices. Small wonder the Bosch turned a machine gun on. He only got one man in the hand, though.

After that the thing became a farce. The bombers, who were new to the place, had to be guided in by their pseudo-Hun, i.e. me.

I suppose you'll be in B'ham at the end of this month, won't you? Because there is just the faintest chance of my people returning to Redditch before I come home again. So I shall possibly be able to come & see you if you feel like receiving me. But don't build on it, I don't want to disappoint you again. As you see, my wretched pen's run out. So I think I'll make that & lunch-time an excuse to stop.

    Cheero, Edith, Girl.

       In hopes, your

         Geoff.

                      R.E.

                      B.E.F.

                   19/4/16

Dearest,

A thousand thanks for the cigarettes & socks. The latter are perfectly ripping, I'm wearing 'em now, those long ones are just the right thing for top-boots, which are quite de rigeur out here at the moment, & at home too, I expect. Fashions in the trenches! Lord! What a war it is! I'm an absolute rotter not to have written & thanked you before & no excuses on earth are plausible enough to condone such a crime. However, I'll endeavour to expiate by sending a little mascot which I have acquired & which will, I hope, find favour in thine eyes.

A week ago a rather higher job started to harass me. Now, like Arthur, I can speak of "my subs", though scarcely in the haughty terms, which you say he uses, as they are all older than I, & all engineers in civil life. So you see my exhalted [*sic*] position is extremely precarious.

You had some perfectly absurd ideas in your last letter about my losing interest in you, because you were slightly younger than I. Why, my dear child, (since you would seemingly have it so) I'm the second youngest officer in the company, & there are twenty-odd of them, so I can hardly think of anything more interesting than to find there's someone even younger than I. Which may sound involved, but means well.

Got a most heart breaking letter from my people, in which they said they weren't going home till the middle of May, & as my leave was due for the beginning, it looked as though we shouldn't see one another this time. Fortunately all leave's been stopped for a time, which should put things right.

My hair is almost going white with worry, but I manage to keep it the right colour with the assistance of a little peroxide. It's the new job, you know. When I'm in trenches the real enemy is behind, a horrible *bête noir* [*sic*] which assumes the shape of working parties which are promised (& of course don't turn up), material, cooking work reports, & quarrelling with the infantry company commander of the trench, who is a G'dsman & probably a duke for all I know. Fearful swank to quarrel with a duke, what! 'Fraid I'm not very tactful with these people.

Well, girl, I'm absolutely 'off' the writing mood so I'll stop drivelling.

Cheero!

Geoff.

177th Co. R.E.
B.E.F.
24 . 4 . 16

Dear Edith,

There's a faint hope.

I MAY be in Redditch for a week commencing May 2nd.

Yrs.

Geoff.

Telephone
Edgbaston 632

Beechcroft
1, Beech Lanes
Birmingham
27 . 4 . 16

Dearest,

I simply love the little mascot – you've no idea how much. It's simply gorgeous and you're far too nice to have sent it to me. I look and look and look at it and already it has become very dear to me. Thank you a thousand times and even that isn't enough. It will be a real mascot – for you. I should imitate the ancient Egyptians and send you a charm against the evil Eye – of the Huns. But this will do instead, won't it? I'll wear it – I'm wearing it now – and it's virtue for good-luck will go out to you. (A little lady-bird has just crawled across this page. That's for luck isn't it? A scarab, don't they call it in Egypt? It's crawled onto my finger. I must be careful with it.)

I've just got a beautiful new perfume. Can you smell it and do you like it? I couldn't resist the name – 'Fleurs d'amour'. Someone of a very practical and botanical turn of mind asked me what 'order' Fleurs d'amour belonged to. The nearest thing that I could suggest was 'Amarillidaceae'! I don't suppose you study Botany out in the trenches though. Still the perfume ought to be very sweet with such a name, don't you think so?

We had a little excitement the other day in the shape of a telegram from the War Office. It wasn't really bad and we are awfully relieved. It said that Arthur was wounded but had remained on duty. This morning we had a cablegram from Arthur himself saying that his wound had healed and that he was resting. Mr. Collins and nearly all the other officers in his company were wounded the week before.

Dear old thing, you have done awfully well. How <u>did</u> you manage it. I'm bucked to death. I think it's perfectly wonderful. I can imagine you coming back with a novelistic iron jaw, and two perpendicular lines in the middle of your forehead, but you mustn't be too fierce and stern. You'll have to develop two thin lines instead of lips to be true to your part. Perhaps if you gave the lordly G'dsman my – er – kind regards he might be more tractable!

By the way in his wanderings, my dear brother came across the place where the Garden of Eden was supposed to have been. Just fancy! He looked about vigorously [*sic*] for some apple trees but couldn't find any!!! He must have been very disappointed, n'est ce pas?

It's getting darker and darker. I'm writing this in the gloaming and the firelight is playing with the shadows on the walls. It looks so sweet. I do wish you were here. This is my favourite dream time so I think I'll stop just for a little while. . . . . The shadows have all gone and the pictures that one imagines in the dusk, so I'll continue.

I didn't go up to London after all, but instead had a topping time rusticating, ruminating or vegetating – which you like, – in the depths of the country. I went with four friends and I'm afraid we excited great consternation in the neighbourhood. Considering that we all "flapped" with large, chic bows and also discarded hats it was really no wonder. On our first journey of exploration we failed to find the village but discovered on closer search that we had walked through it, unfortunately not having noticed it. There was one shop, besides the butcher's, so we bombarded it in force. The unfortunate part was that when we ran short of ribbon etc. the only means of getting any more, was to commission the bus boy who came through about twice weekly to purchase some at the nearest town. Just imagine sending a mere male to buy ribbons and laces!

'nuff said!

The village blacksmith – the most weird looking object I've ever seen – fell in love with us and presented us all with horseshoes. I hope he didn't think we belonged to that species of quadruped! Unfortunately we all fell in love with butcher, who, sad to relate had a wife and babe, so the blacksmith wasn't in the running. So that the country shouldn't absolutely go to the beast of the canine tribe, we had an argument one night as to how affairs should be carried on, but the only conclusion that was arrived at with general satisfaction to the whole assembly was that the butcher ought to be Prince of Wales!!! I'm afraid that in spite of his seraphic looks he swindled us beautifully.

We had 'some' Rector, too. He startled us considerably by informing us that 'God made the country, man made the town and the devil made the suburbs!!!' He sounded as though he knew a lot about it, didn't he?

In our ramblings we found the sweetest little village imaginable. Just such a place as you would have loved "when you were a nice quiet little boy", – how long ago? I absolutely fell in love with it. Especially as I discovered my dream cottage where I'm going to bring my dog and parrot when I'm 'through'. It had a dear little Japanese garden with fruit blossom in full bloom. It was so quaint. I don't think you could suggest anything much nicer than living there.

Dear, I'm so sorry about the leave. Anyway it only means another month of anticipation, doesn't it? Let's not talk about it any more and then perhaps it may come sooner. Shall's? Although it <u>is</u> rather nice to talk about it, isn't it?

I read the other day that

> "If you're good you're not good-looking.
> If good-looking you're not good."

That's very sad isn't it? I've been thinking hard ever since wondering which I'd rather be. I've come to the conclusion that it's possible to be neither!

    Well, Goodbye, dear one.
     À toi, cher.
      Edith

         <u>27/4/16</u>
         Trenches..

Dearest,

Leave postponed about a week. Will probably be in Brum somewhere near May 9th with luck.

The hope I mentioned is now far stronger, but please don't build too many castles in the air. I should hate to disappoint again.

    Yrs.
     Geoff.

Telephone
Edgbaston 632

Beechcroft
1, Beech Lanes
Birmingham
4.5.16

Geoff, dearest,

I'm not going to write much because we <u>may</u> be able to say all we want next week. You see I'm keeping to the 'may' and I'm not indulging in any unnecessary day-dreams – or at least I'm trying not to.

I can't really believe that you're coming yet but I hope and hope and hope. Do, do be careful just for a week and let's hope the Fates will be indulgent for once.

You won't come unexpectedly will you? You see if I were to meet you accidentally in New St. and you didn't recognise me I should be most annoyed!! Probably I shouldn't speak to you again – which would be most sad. So do let me know so that I can guard against such a catastrophe.

I wonder if you are half as excited as I am?

I have to go and regale the Music Man with weird noises now. So Goodbye – only for a week though, I hope.

Edith.

*Copies of telegrams in Geoffrey's service record held at the
National Archives. File WO339/5068, reproduced by permission.*

POST OFFICE TELEGRAPHS.

(Inland Official) Telegrams only.)

No. of Telegram

I certify that this Telegram is sent on the service of the

O.H.M.S.

(Signature) P Parker

Attention is called to the Regulations printed at the back hereof

Dated Stamp.

TO { Boothby charlemont West Bromwich.

Deeply regret to inform you 2Lt C. G. Boothby
RE was killed in action April 28th Lord
Kitchener expresses his sympathy.

FROM { SECRETARY, WAR OFFICE.

Name and Address of the Sender, IF NOT TO BE TELEGRAPHED, should be written in the space provided at the Back of the Form.

Charles Boothby's disbelieving response to the news of Geoffrey's death,
"I cannot think it true please confirm," with the confirmation below.

BIRMINGHAM DAILY MAIL, TUESDAY MAY 9, 1916

LATEST CASUALTIES

OVER 900 NAMES IN LAST NIGHT'S LIST

WORCESTER OFFICER KILLED

The casualty lists issued last night contained the names of 73 officers (16 dead, 53 wounded and missing) and 830 non-commissioned officers and men (258 dead and 572 wounded and missing).

The rank and file list includes the following losses in the Australian, Newfoundland, and South African forces: Killed 37, died of wounds 21, died 27, wounded 95, missing 1; total 181.

Among the officers killed is Second-Lieut. Boothby, South Staffs., attached R.E.

Information has been received at Hales Owen that Lieutenant Charles Hill, a son of the Rev. J. C. Hill, rector of Bury, who for fifteen years was rector of Hales Owen, is reported missing.

28/4/16

1

(M.S.3.Cas.)

8th June, 1916.

The Military Secretary presents his
compliments to Mr. Chas. Boothby and begs to inform
him that a report has just been received which states
that the place where the late 2nd Lieutenant C. G.
Boothby, Royal Engineers, was killed in action was
near Ypres (Reference to Map. Sheet 28. I.C.3.9.)

The Military Secretary much regrets that the
body was not recovered.

T3. 2090

597/2

C. Boothby Esq
Park View
Aslwood Bank
Redditch

F.V.3/3281/0

CEMETERY REGISTERS.

The whole of this form should be filled up to the RIGHT OF CENTRAL LINE and returned as early as possible to the address printed on the back. The form requires no postage stamp and can be folded on the lines marked.

PLEASE WRITE CLEARLY.

CEMETERY *Railway Wood Zillebeke*

Surname ... ... *BOOTHBY*

Rank ... ... *Second Lieutenant*

Christian or Forenames (in full)... *Charles Geoffrey.*

Regimental Number ... ...

Military Honours ... ...

Particulars of Company, Battery, etc , and, in case of Naval Units, the name of the ship should be given ... ...

Regiment ... ... *177ª Tun Co Royal Engineers*

Nature of death (if desired and if particulars are available)...

Date of death ... ... *28ª April 1916*

Age *21 years*

Give both parents, and native place of soldier (if desired)
Son of *Charles & Alice Boothby England*

Husband of

Wife's address (if desired) ...

Any other particulars in reference to soldier (if desired) ...

Plot ... ...
Row ... ... *R.E. Grave*
Grave ... ...

PLEASE WRITE CLEARLY.

(Signed) *Alice Boothby* ... Relationship *Mother*

Address *Park View Astwood Bank Nr Redditch*

(954). Wt. 24600/W865. 50,000. 5/22. **146** F. & S.

Extracts from letters to Alice Boothby
from officers who had served with Geoffrey
(Edith copied these out by hand)

[no address or date]

Dear Mrs Boothby,

I am more sorry than I can express to have to send you some very bad news, in fact the worst, of your son, ii Lieut. Boothby.

I regret to say that he, with 2 other men, was in a part of one of our mines when the enemy fired a camouflet[3] on 28th April. The only consolation is that they must have been killed absolutely instantaneously and painlessly.

He was a most likeable man and a very keen and efficient officer, and both I and all my officers feel his loss very deeply, both on the social and military counts. We wish to ask you to accept our most sincere sympathy.

I regret to say that it has been impossible to retrieve his body for proper burial and I am unable by letter, or from this country to give you any further details. But I am making my H.Q. at the J.V.S. Club, Charles St. from the 12th to the 20th inst, and would gladly give you any further information. . . .

With deepest sympathy,
Yours sincerely,
J. M. Bliss,
Major R.E.

8th Btn., South Staffordshire Reg't

B.E.F.   12th May 1916

Dear Mrs Boothby,

Owing to the fact that your son had left the Batt'n it was only a day or two ago that we heard the very sad news of his death. He was very popular in this Batt'n and the news has been received with the profoundest regret by all of us who knew him. On behalf of the Commanding Officer, who is away on leave, I write to express to you and yours our very great sympathy in your sorrow. Your son from the <u>very</u> first proved himself to be an extremely keen and capable officer and when he came out here he showed himself to be as courageous as he was capable. We were all very disappointed that he did not get decorated for a very plucky bit of work which he did last Oct. when he was acting as mining officer in our trenches. Unfortunately the officer just senior to him got the decoration though I have always understood that your son was chiefly responsible for the work done on that occasion —Anyway he risked his life to prevent the enemy blowing up a mine which was laid under part of our trench and succeeded in preventing it. He will aways be remembered by us in this Batt'n as a very gallant officer and a very upright clean-minded English gentleman.

Yours very sincerely,

R. G. Raper. Major.

22/5/16

The Grange
Butterly, Derby.

My Dear Mrs Boothby,

. . . I was with your son ever since our Brigade arrived in France and were both in charge of the Brigade mining section from St Eloi, where we first went into trenches till we got to the right of Hooge called ——. Here we were attached to the 177 Coy. R.E., who were very good to us as they were short of officers they asked us to transfer which we did. We both were working as R.E. till our transfer came through and then as soon as some of the senior officers got promoted and left the company we got charge of jobs. Your son Geoffrey was in charge at —— and I was put in charge of other work at a different part of the line. I can say that everybody thought a great deal of your son from the O.C. down to the junior subaltern as he always had a smile on his face and feared nothing. Although he did not know much about mining before the war it speaks well seeing that he was put in charge of the great workings at —— in just over six months work – it was nothing but bad luck and a great loss to the company that so young and fearless an officer was killed. How it happened was like this, although I was not there at the time I have heard it from the officers who were on the job at the time. The officer on the night shift was called to investigate some noises of the enemy working and did so but was not allowed to "blow", as the officer in charge of this job has to do that and besides the noises were not near enough, so he thought. So he went down and called your son about 6 in the morning, and they went to the mine together, your son in front with the Corporal with the other officer a little way behind. No sooner had your son got to the face than the enemy blew their mine and buried your son and the Corporal, while the shock of the explosion blew the other officer away. Death was of course instantaneous. The other officer recovered enough to get help and three times went to the place of the blow but was overcome by gas each time and could only see there was no hope of ever getting the bodies out. Everybody was dumbfounded when they heard the news in camp and everybody misses his cheery smile which always helped to cheer everybody up in our camp, and with his death the 177th Company as well as the British Army have lost a very fine young and cheerful officer. With all my sympathy to you in your bereavement I bring this long epistle to a close and hope I have explained everthing fairly well to you, but my one hope is that I can be half as cheerful and fearless as your son who was my best friend out here.

   Yours very sincerely,
    Montague F. M. Wright
     2 Lieut 177 Coy R.E.

             South Elmsall
             Nr. Pontefract
             [no date]

Dear Mrs Boothby,

  I am very deeply touched by your letter of thanks and I am sorry that what I did was of so little effect.

  The explosion occurred about 7 A.M.

  It was reported to me about 6.45 a.m. that the workers at the face had heard sounds of talking coming through the earth and when I went to investigate I was of the same opinion.

  I stopped the working in that part of the mine to avoid risk of our detection and went immediately to our C.O. to put the matter before him, for it is the custom in tunnelling for the less experienced to report to the officer in charge if time permits, to get the benefit of his experience and help.

  I found your boy just getting up and when I told him what had occurred he decided to go up with me at once and slipped into his long boots. On our way up to the mine we discussed the situation and he said there was no need to take definite action until we were quite sure, as he was very much against alarming the men until there could be no possibility of a mistake about it, and he pointed out that as the talking was so unguarded there was every possibility that our men had not been heard by the Germans.

It was just that self-reliance and careful weighing of facts and absence of flurry that made him so valuable to his junior officers and the men.

He went at once to the suspected gallery, taking with him to the head of the gallery the man who had reported the sounds.

As the gallery was very small and a third listener would have been in the way I stood at the entrance of the gallery to ensure quiet in the main gallery during the listening.

About half a minute later the explosion occurred and as soon as I could get clear of the wreckage I sent a man back to get help and went in to see the extent of the damage. I found the gallery entirely blocked for almost the whole length with earth and broken timbers, and was almost immediately made insensible by the fumes. From the severity of explosion and the fact that he was so near the seat of it - apart altogether from the absence of air – your boy's death must have been immediate, and I know he would be ready.

I know I express the feelings of the officers and men of the company in saying how deeply we shall miss his quiet confidence and cheerful coolness, and we share with you the loss of a very brave and gallant gentleman.

Believe me,

Alex W. Wilson, 2nd Lieut. R.E.[4]

P.S. My wounds are healing very well indeed, and the doctor thinks that I shall be quite well again in 3 or 4 months if I take care of myself

Yours sincerely,

A. W. W.

Extract from a letter to Mrs Boothby from Geoffrey's school headmaster

Cla}esmore School
Northwood Park
Winchester
7th July 1916

My dear Mrs Boothby,

. . . I did see your dear boy's name on the list of the killed, and it plunged me in great distress and at the same time filled my heart with pride for him. He was indeed a dear boy; we loved him here at school very sincerely, and always regretted that somehow he did not keep in touch with his old school, but he was, as you know, a very undemonstrative soul. We often talked of him and wondered how he was doing, and then one day he was passing the school and saw the name on the gates and came in and spent an evening with me, and was as jolly and affectionate as ever, and so I saw that his long silence was not due to any lack of regard, but probably to a dislike of letter-writing or making a fuss. He was quartered quite near us – in fact adjoining our Estate and it was a great joy to see him. I did not know when he was going and could not say good-bye to him, and the next news we had of him was that he had died on the field of honour.

[*the next two paragraphs refer to inscribing his name in the school war memorial*]

You do not know what a warm place I had in my heart for him. I dare say he did not know himself or else we should have heard more of him. I can well understand all you feel. I know how dear he was to you and his father and I know what you have given up for England and for all of us in the person of your brave boy. It is difficult to put into words all one has in one's heart of pity for you and yet pride in the boy.

[*In the next paragraph he proposes to write about him in the school magazine, the* Clayesmorian]

Please give my kindest regards to Mr Boothby, and I pray God may console and comfort you in your anguish. What a dear boy he was, and how better can a man die or live than to do as he has done, but that does not heal your wound, does it?

With warmest regards,

Believe me to remain,

Yours sincerely,

Alex Devine.

Notes

1. An obstacle, typically made of wood, covered with barbed wire or spikes, used to block the advancing enemy . . . it was derived from the French for "horse of Friesland", so named because it was first used by Frisians who lacked cavalry. [anu@wordsmith.org]

2. It seems that they narrowly missed each other when Edith went to Bournemouth. I have two snapshots, dated and annotated in Arthur's handwriting. On the one is written: "Lt. Davis in fancy bathing costume. Preiss [?] hut, Bournemouth, Sunday 18–7–15." On the other is the annotation: "Outside my hut. Bovington Camp. G, E. and Lts Davis and Iles. 19–7–15." On the second photo, Lts Davis and Iles are standing in the doorway of the hut, while Edith's sister Gladys, and Edith herself are standing to either side, wearing hats, long dresses and white gloves! Lt. Davis seems to be a droll character. At any rate, this proves that Edith was at Bovington Camp on 19th July 1915. But by 26th July (see next letter) Geoffrey writes from France that he has marched his men a long distance on cobbled roads. He regrets that he did not have two days longer in England. The photos also demonstrate that Geoffrey and Arthur must have been at Bovington Camp at the same time.

3. A French word normally meaning a "snub". But according to *Larousse* it is also used in the technical military sense of an explosive charge designed to destroy a subterranean gallery in the hands of the enemy (*fourneau de mine destiné à écraser une galerie souterraine adverse*)

4. He is clearly the "other officer" referred to by Lieutenant Wright.

Alice Boothby's farewell

Will you come back when The Tide Turns?
After many days? My heart yearns
To know!
And so I seem
To have you still the same
In one world with me
As if it were part and parcel,
One shadow, And we need not dissemble
Our darkness: do you understand?

For I have Told you plain how it is —

I shall always wonder over you, and look for you —
And you will always be with me —

Geoffrey as a schoolboy

The Epilogue

Versions of an incident

Geoffrey wrote three versions of the incident when a German telephone was found in a British tunnel. One was to Edith, in his letter of 13th October 1915. The second was longer, written to his parents about the same time, and much later reproduced in his school magazine, the *Clayesmorian*, for December 1916, some nine months after he had died. A third was a short account in a letter to his school headmaster, Mr Alex Devine. It is not clear when Geoffrey wrote it, but it was reproduced in the *Clayesmorian* for April 1916. Even though these letters duplicate much of his letter to Edith, they differ somewhat in content and style, the second one also including some new material. I reproduce them below in full.

AN ADVENTURE IN A GERMAN MINE-SHAFT

[A melancholy interest attaches to the following narrative, which is taken from a home-letter from the late Lieut. C.G. Boothby, O.C., whose death at the Front is noticed elsewhere. – Ed. Clayesmorian]

About eight days ago I left the R.E. Company to which I was attached, and proceeded with Brigade Mining Section to a new lot of trenches, there to take over the mines.

Though this was only a few yards from one of the hottest mining sectors in the whole line, the mines we took over were reported to be very quiet and peaceful by the miners who handed them over to us. Quiet and peaceful! I should smile! But here is the story.

I've been in the fighting line about two months now, and only a couple of days ago did I have my first real adventure, the first worth mentioning in my so long tranquil existence. The mines were handed over to two of us officers and one Brigade Section. I took two and the other officer[1] the other two. Well, after we had been there two days, an R.E. officer came up to look round. He went down my two and found them all correct. Then he went down the other two with the officer in charge. Out of curiosity he went along an old gallery half full of water. Imagine their surprise when they suddenly came upon an instrument like an enlarged telephone receiver stuck in the wall, and connected up with wires which ran along the gallery in front of them into the darkness. Upon examination this thing was found to have German words on it. They disconnected the wires and took the instrument out to the open air without going further along the gallery. I was waiting at the top, and got a pretty shock when I saw what they had found.

Of course, it didn't require a Sherlock to deduce that the wily Bosch had broken into this old gallery further along than the spot where they had found the instrument. So the three of us decided to explore and find where the Huns had got in. Now, so that you can fully appreciate the situation, I will inform you that our galleries are just like a square tube in the earth, going down straight and then shooting out and running parallel to the surface of the ground about twenty feet down underground. These galleries measure four feet by three, so you're pretty cramped. In this old gallery there was about eighteen inches of water.

Well, down we went and along through the water, until we came to the Germans' gallery. This was properly joined up with ours, and must have been done long before we took over the mines. Just in the Huns' gallery there was a water pump, which they were using to pump water into our sap, so that they could hear us coming through the water and thus be ready for us. There was also the rest of the telegraphic apparatus, a beautiful and complicated piece of workmanship in a mahogany box about 2½ft. long. The instrument, by the way, was a kind of wireless, by means of which they could tap the wires from our front trenches running back to headquarters, big guns, etc., a very useful weapon in the hands of the crafty Bosch.

As we only had one rifle between us, we thought it rather dangerous to explore more than a few yards of the German gallery, so we cleared out and at the top began to make things fly, sending for explosives, etc. Then three of us went down again – the R.E. officer, a corporal, and little me. Two rifles this time. Our object was to get the rest of the instrument, which we'd left in the first place for fear the Huns should come, and finding it gone, give the alarm before we were ready to blow him up. So along we went – me first with a rifle and flash lamp, followed by the corporal, the

R.E. officer in the rear. The water made a horrible noise round our legs, as it was up to the knee. The gallery had a slight bend in it, and when we had rounded this and were in the straight into which the German gallery ran at right angles, suddenly – as the novels and penny hair-raisers say – 'a shot rang out'! As a matter of fact it didn't ring at all, but made a business-like 'porp!' I had to drop the lamp to work my rifle, and managed to get one shot off, but the other two retreated. Of course it was useless to stay any longer, as the Bosch had us absolutely. You see, he was in a dry gallery and right round the corner, his revolver poked into our gallery, and firing at random without exposing himself at all. And here I must tell you that the Hebrew spirit is strong within me, for I dropped the rifle and groped in the water for my torch while he got two more shots off, my sole thought being 'Dash, there goes a guinea.' Then I beat an absolutely panic-stricken retreat, dashing through the water, bent double to avoid the roof, and crashing from side to side. It was, you realise, quite dark. I got to the others at the next corner round the bend, about fifteen yards from the German sap, and found the corporal had lost his rifle too. So the R.E. officer went up to the surface, while the corporal and I stayed on guard in the dark. A rifle came down and my revolver, which had arrived at last. Then we made things hum. Men all along the galleries behind us dragging full sandbags along and leaving them for us to build a barricade. I boarded up the corner we were holding, then piled sandbags behind. Then the explosives were sent down, and the corporal packed sandbags round it and filled our own gallery with sandbags six feet back from the charge. This has to be done so that the explosion goes forward and not back into your own gallery. My word! How we worked. It took the corporal and I [sic] four hours to get the whole thing ready for firing. The sandbags had to be dragged through water to us, and consequently we were absolutely wringing, and then the heat and bad air, phew! The object of this haste was to get our charge off before the Germans got off theirs and buried us. About the toughest race I've run yet.

Doubtless they were working as hard as we, but we won. The explosion made a twelve-yard crater on the surface.

General Staff seemed rather bucked.[2]

The third account, sent to Mr Devine, is short and to the point.

Lieut. G. Boothby, 8th South Staffordshires, sends us a very interesting and exciting account of his life at the Front. He says:

You will be pleased to hear that I have a 'manual labour' billet with a vengeance. All of us here are manual labourers to a certain extent, but I have gone one better. My job is that of Brigade Mining Officer, and, together with another officer and a handful of mud-plastered villains, I endeavour to outwit the wily Bosch underground, and now and again elevate that personage sky-high with a well-placed charge of powder.

The job is rather interesting, and affords at long intervals quite exciting little periods, as instanced by a short and sharp 'strafe',[3] we enjoyed a couple of weeks ago. We took over several shafts from another Brigade Mining Section, and while examining two galleries came upon a microphone stuck in the wall of an old heading, which was half full of water. Further exploration showed us that the Hun had connected his gallery up with ours, and had established a listening post at the junction. We found a complicated electrical instrument and a water-pump, with which he used to pump the water from his gallery into ours. Well, we left these while we went to hustle around above ground and get explosives ready. Then three of us, an R.E. Officer, a corporal, and I went down to bag the thing. Mr Hun was ready for us, though, and let off rapid with a revolver at six yards range. These galleries are 4ft. by 3ft., so this was a wee bit unhealthy, especially as the Bosch was completely concealed behind a right-angled corner. So after firing one shot with my rifle, I retired ungracefully to the next corner, where, together with the corporal, I built a barricade, and laid a charge which the R.E. officer fired. This little job took us four hours, and was rather exciting, as the Hun was doing precisely the same thing. However, we got ours off first, and I'm afraid the Bosch was decidedly an 'also ran' on that occasion.

Otherwise, mining is a peaceful business. We dig a bit, and listen a bit, and everything is very nice. . . . until we hear the Bosch digging too.[4]

What is striking in these accounts is their clarity and descriptive power. His language and style communicate a graphic and powerful impression, not without a certain black humour. He also knows how to tailor his description to different audiences. To Edith he retails intriguing tidbits, such as the word "unten" that proves the telephone instrument is German, the muffled sound that a rifle shot makes in a tunnel, and the failed scramble to find his expensive torch, ending with: "Some sport! What!" To his parents he provides even more detail, describing for instance the rationale behind the sandbagging operation prior to a "blow". And he nicely concludes: "General Staff seemed rather bucked." To Mr Devine he is straight and matter-of-fact, if in places ironic, as with the qualified statement: "Otherwise, mining is a peaceful business," In one of her letters Edith discusses future careers and asks him, among other things, if he would write books. Perhaps she was not far off the mark.

Where Geoffrey was

All letters from the front were subject to censorship. Presumably Geoffrey was not allowed to say in his letters from France and Belgium where he was at any particular time. He makes no secret of the fact that for most of his service he was in Belgium, and there are several references to Ypres. But no other location is mentioned by name. Files at the National Archives, however, give us some indication of his movements.

We know from the letters that he crossed the Channel to France at a date between 11th and 26th July 1915,[5] with the South Staffordshire Regiment. By 11th August he must have been at or close to the front, but he may have arrived there by 26th July, since in his letter of that date he writes of a tough march for his men, suggesting that they went a considerable distance from the coast. On 26th August he refers to "the RE [*Royal Engineers*] Coy to which I am attached". This must be the 172nd RE Coy. The entry in the Company diary for 21st August refers to "2 officers and 35 ORs [*other ranks*] 51st Bde. Mining section attached for instruction".[6] In Geoffrey's letter of 14th September, he writes that he is "attached to the 172 Coy R.E. for tunnelling duty", since his "Brigade Mining Section and another have been amalgamated and placed at the disposal of the 172 Coy". His letter of 21st December is headed "Mining Section, 51st Inf. Brigade, B.E.F." But on 13th October he writes: "I left the R.E. some time ago & went with my trusty miners to the trenches occupied by our Brigade, there to take over the mines." Then he recounts the adventure of the German telephonic apparatus. Here we are able for the first time to pin down just where he was, since the Diary of the 172nd R.E. Coy, in its entry of 5th October, reports that:

Lt. Williamson while making inspection of defence galleries in trenches 32 and 33 discovered German listening apparatus fixed in our gallery. Found that Germans had connected into our gallery the disconnected listening apparatus & sent for explosive. While exploring further he and two other officers were fired at by the enemy. They retired behind a bend & placed charge & blew in the gallery. Casualties nil.[7]

From this we know the name of the R.E. officer referred to by Geoffrey in his letters. But we also know from the Diary that this operation took place at St Elooi (French spelling St Eloi), which is more or less at the southern extremity of the Salient, due south of Ieper. We may also speculate that when he went to a Pierrot show in "a certain town near at hand most of the houses of which are standing",[8] he went to Poperinge, about 9 km west of Ieper, since this was far enough from the front line to escape most of the shelling, was still in Belgium (just) and was much used for rest and recreation.

Geoffrey's letter of 22nd January 1916 is the first to bear the address of 177th Tunnelling Coy. Subsequently the address becomes less specific, and it is not till 20th March that he announces that: "My transfer's come through at last & I'm a real R.E." He writes that he has been posted to the company he has been with for the last five months, so that "S. Staffs attached" need no longer appear on his address. The Diary of the 177th Tunnelling Coy notes that on 18th March Lts. Boothby and Wright joined them that day.[9] For an indefinite period up to this point, therefore, he appears to have had some sort of probationary status as a tunneller. He has been attached to the 172nd Tunnelling Coy., to the Mining Section of the 51st Infantry Brigade until finally he is fully part of the 177th Tunnelling Coy. It is not entirely clear when the earlier transitions took place.

In the Diary of the 177th there is a Weekly Mine Report, dated April 1916. It is headed "14th Corps, Guards Division":

Intend to replace end of 11G. End of Gallery was probably immediately over the enemy Gallery. Enemy were heard on morning of 28th and blew a camouflet at 7.45 a.m. 2nd Leiut. Boothby and 2 O.R. were in 11 H and were killed and buried in there. 11 H and the last 40' of 11G were wrecked by the explosion. II Lieut. Wilson and 4 O.R. more or less severely injured.

The camouflet was blown at Railway Wood, a little north of the Menin Road, approximately 4 km to the east of Ieper.

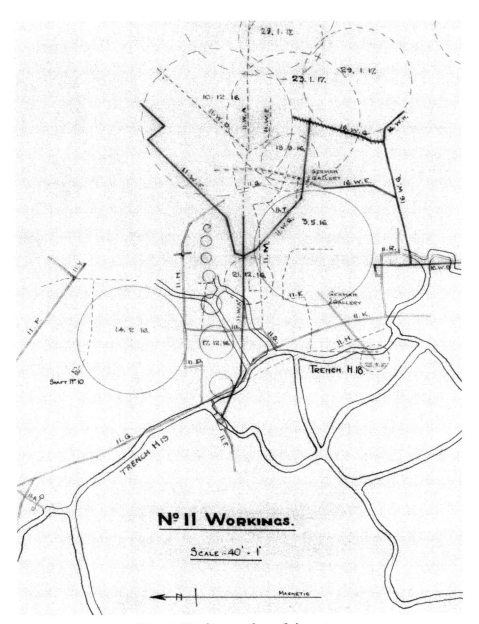

No. 11 Workings: plan of the mines,
by courtesy of the Royal Engineers Library.

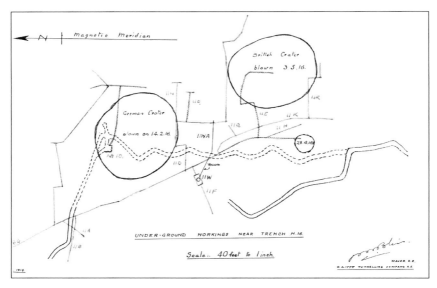

*Detail showing location of the explosion that killed
Geoffrey and his comrades on 28th April 1916, 7.45 a.m.,
by courtesy of the Royal Engineers Library.*

The Survivors

What happened to those who were left in this story after Geoffrey's death? Most of the protagonists were very young or in early middle age, so that they could expect many years of life ahead of them. Geoffrey, had he survived, might have lived into the 1960s or 1970s, assuming an average span.

Edith, who was three years younger, went on to graduate in Medicine from Birmingham University. She was, by all accounts, a lively undergraduate. A brief correspondence survives between her and the Vice-Chancellor of the University, Sir Oliver Lodge, in which she had to apologise on behalf of the women students for some (unspecified) student prank. After graduation (MB, ChB, 1920; DPH [*Diploma of Public Health*], 1925), she went into general medicine, and was employed for a number of years at Birmingham's General Hospital, work she greatly

Edith as a young woman

enjoyed. A successful job application that she made in September 1927 lists past and present appointments as follows:

Casualty House Surgeon, General Hospital, Birmingham. House Surgeon to Mr Lucas, FRCS, General Hospital, Birmingham. House Physician to Dr Wynn, Professor of Medicine, General Hospital, Birmingham. Resident Medical Officer in charge of the whole of the medical side of the General Hospital, Birmingham. Part Time Assistant Medical Officer to Infant Welfare Clinics, Smethwick. Visiting Anaesthetist, General Hospital, Birmingham. Stipendiary Anaesthetist, Dental Hospital, Birmingham. Lecturer, tutor and examiner in Dental Anaesthetics, Birmingham University.

Under "additional information" she states that the post of Resident Medical Officer (which she held for two years) meant being "responsible for the whole organisation of the Medical side of the General Hospital", and that the holder "is the Senior Medical Officer with full responsibility for all the wards and the Junior Resident Medical Staff in the absence of Honorary Physicians. The Children's Wards are under the special charge of the R.M.O. This post provides unique training in organisation, as well as a wide medical experience."

The position she obtained was that of full time Assistant Medical Officer of Health for the County Borough of Smethwick[10]

She continued to live at home with her parents in Bearwood, but during holiday periods was able to go on cruises, to the Mediterranean, the Baltic and once as far north as Spitzbergen (Svalbard). In April 1934 – nearly 18 years after Geoffrey's death – she married Wilfred Stockwin, a dentist who had graduated from the same university. They bought together a big old Victorian house in Sutton Coldfield, then a 'Royal Town' on the north-eastern fringe of Birmingham (into which it was much later incorporated) where Wilfred set up his dental practice. Edith, who was required to give up her salaried position on marriage: an unenlightened custom of those days, started to work part time at ante-natal and post-natal clinics in the area. Her knowledge of anaesthetics also allowed her to act as Wilfred's anaesthetist. For many years she was an active member (at times an official) of the Birmingham Medical Women's Association.

Some eighteen months after her marriage, her first and only child was born (myself). During the years 1940–2, when Birmingham was being heavily bombed, she took me with her to board with a family in the Shropshire village of Edgmond, and I remember that time, between the ages of four and six, as an idyllic, almost carefree existence, which gave me an abiding love of the countryside. It must have been less easy for my parents. My father remained at his practice, but visited us fairly frequently at weekends. Even so peaceful a place was not entirely untouched by war. One evening an aircraft flew low over our rooftops and ditched in a field not far away. The military police were on the spot with great speed, and took the German pilot prisoner.

Edith in middle age

A few years later, when the war was just about over, my mother took me a few times to Stratford-upon-Avon, where in the suburb of Shottery we would visit a very old lady, whose health was poor. So far as I ever thought about it, my mother seemed to visit her partly as a doctor, and partly as a family friend. I was mostly allowed to play outside, and all I remember of the house was that it was rambling and dark. But I recall one thing quite vividly. Set into the living room mantelpiece was a black metal plaque, no doubt standard War Office issue, commemorating a soldier killed in the First World War. The soldier had been the son of my mother's friend, and the name on the plaque was Geoffrey Boothby. I must have remarked upon it to my mother later, because I remember her telling me that Mrs Boothby was sad because she had lost her son, but that was all she ever said about it, then or at any later time.

Edith had a full and productive life, and survived to an advanced age, but her last years were blighted by advancing senility. She died in 1983 at the home she had lived in for 49 years. When Geoffrey, in one of his letters to her, speculated on what they would be like in their sixties, he could hardly have envisaged that she would outlive him by more than 60 years.

What of the other characters in this saga?

Edith's brother Arthur – Geoff's close friend – survived the war, and then, like most of the rest of his family, graduated in medicine. But the war, while sparing him, had twisted his soul. After graduation, he entered into partnership with his father in general practice in the family home. As Geoffrey had feared might be his own lot, Arthur was incensed by the fact that some of his contemporaries, who had managed to avoid military service, had been able to steal a march on him in career terms. It may also be the case that, as the only son – and born before another son died in infancy – in a family where the other children were girls, he was over-protected by his parents, especially his mother. This was no doubt accentuated by the fact that he was the only one of them to go to war. Remember how Edith wrote in a letter what a fuss they would make of Arthur if he came back on leave. Then once the war was over and he had qualified, he was able to walk straight into a share in his father's practice, without having to struggle to set up his own.

Some time in the late 1920s Arthur married and had four children with his wife, having set up house not far from his parents' home. When they had been married a decade or so there was a terrible divorce case. He sought refuge in alcohol, though his drinking seems to have been part of the reason for the failure of his marriage. He lived until 25th November 1961, but in his last years was practically a derelict, and he succeeded in making my mother's life a misery for nearly two decades from the Second World War.

Gloomy though the thought may be, I cannot help wondering which is worse – to be cut off in one's prime, like Geoff, or survive and live one's later years as a twisted alcoholic and grumbler, being a nuisance to all around. But Arthur was not all bad, by any means. Two letters from him survive, from which I quote extracts. The first describes the camp at Wool in Dorset, where both young men were stationed before going to the war.

[no address or date; page 1 missing]

. . . evidently been wandering for the last twelve months. When I got to Wool, I was informed that the Camp was two miles up some "ROAD". I proceeded forthwith and found that it was indeed <u>some</u> road. In my various wanderings never before in my natural [sic] have I been on or seen such a terrific road. It was full of 1 ft. diameter and deep pot holes, huge stones scattered all over the place, dust 1 ft. deep, big ruts where traction engines had proceeded up and down from the camp for the last twelve <u>years</u>. Well, one of my front springs broke as the result. This road is the only way out of the camp. I arrived at the 12th Warwick huts and had dinner, the mess being about half way through. This Camp, called Bovington Camp, is an immense camp, having been a camp before the war. It is well fitted out with most conveniences, such as electric light, Picture Palace, concert hall, several shops, barbers, chemist, photographer, tobacconists, Post office, plenty of canteens. There are about ten Battalions in the camp, practically all in huts. Of course all these shops etc. are huts.

The number of huts runs into several hundreds while the number of men to nearly 10,000. The camp is really beautifully situated amid woods of fir trees with several very pretty rivers and streams round about, and the air is delightful. It would be an ideal place if it were not for being miles from anywhere. Wool, two miles away, has at the most, ten cottages, while Wareham 7 miles away is not much better. Bournemouth is 22 miles away, Weymouth, 18 miles, Swanage 13 miles, Martin is at Swanage. Of course I am at a great advantage with my bike; but oh! that "road" to Wool.

By the way, my total mileage from B'ham down here was at least 180 miles.

We are, as you know, in huts. I am in one large hut with seven others; it is a very nice hut and there is tons of room, they would put about 40 tommies in it. I, being the senior officer in the hut, am in charge of it, the other seven are all ripping chaps, and of course Colley is in. I had no bed the first night so slept on the floor, the next night and last night I managed to borrow one man's who was away. I suppose I shall get my own today and I now thank you for sending it.

The morning after I arrived I was up at 6 o'clock and did an hour's bayonet drill before breakfast; I was attached to the men to instruct them. After breakfast, at 9 o'clock I started with the men and five other officers for a route march, arriving back at 1.30 after doing 13 miles. It was boiling hot and the dust was awful. I really enjoyed it as I felt as fit as a fiddle after it. The sun scorched my neck. . . .   [The rest of the letter is missing]

The second, written in the early 1950s to Edith, when he was already far gone in alcoholism, has its share of paranoia and bitterness (note the initial greeting), but it gives a moving account of what war can do to the people caught up in it, both physically and psychologically:

Llandudno
Saturday 13th May [1950]

Dearest Madam,

In the 1914–1918 war I endured the most profound sufferings of Gallipoli, Mesopotamia, flying etc. in my teens and early twenties. I have kept them for the most part to myself and tried to remember the good times we had which were many and happy. I still frequently think of the men under me – a mere boy – how often my life was saved by them, some of them criminals from Parkhurst Prison who they gave remission of their sentences provided they joined the Warwicks at the Barracks next door. I remember when I took my platoon consisting mostly of these men their first route march and they kept singing "A little child shall lead us, lead us gently on our way." When I got back to Barracks the Adjutant asked me how I got on and I told him fine but that they kept singing "the little child song". He said, how far did you go, and I replied "7 miles". He then said "do you ride a horse?" I said "well, I can stick on one." He then said "take them 14 miles tomorrow and you can have my horse". They almost laughed when I came on the Square next day mounted on a horse, but the Adjutant was watching them so they dare not! I always took them down Sea St. where the Shepherds lived and they always stood at their door to watch me. They turned out to be a grand lot of men. When we set foot on Suvla I was terrified out of my life but not them.

Amongst the officers, every one a good one, I remember Geoffrey at the Staff College when even Mother mistook him for me as he stood at the window awaiting their arrival on a weekend, whilst I was rushing downstairs to greet Mother and Father – I have just forgotten whether you were with them. Those were some of the happy days, to be quickly followed by the horrors of war. . . .

Then there was Haslam, my batman, the maid's brother, who saved my life when I had frost bite following the great flood and blizzard – 7" of rain and sleet in a night and we still in shorts and a shirt. He looked after me like a baby whilst he had the horrible frost bite worse than I did, and died on a hospital ship having had both feet amputated. He was buried at Malta. I have a photo of him somewhere which Alice gave me. . . .

Then came the aftermath of the War, the difficulty of settling down to medicine. . . .

Fondest love
Arthur

It may not be going too far to suggest that Arthur was as much a victim of the First World War as was Geoff, one of them corroded by it over decades, the other killed by it in seconds. For Edith, who had been close to both of them, that war was a spectator's horror, a war far worse than the Second in her view. Until I learned the whole story, long after her death, I never fully realised why she was always so moved when she heard the playing of the 'Last Post'.

For completeness, I must say what happened to Geoff's mysterious "dark cousin", whom he mentions with mock jealousy a few times in the letters. I am nearly certain this was Herbert Pollitt, the son of one of Alice Boothby's two sisters. I never had the opportunity of meeting him, but my mother kept his acquaintance and talked about him from time to time. Apparently he married late, after World War II, and had several children. Alas, he and two or three of his children were killed in a horrible road smash in the mid-1960s.

Alice and Charles Boothby, Geoffrey's parents, had a particularly difficult time after his death. Charles, as is evident from some of Geoffrey's later letters, suffered from a chronic illness, which led him to seek healthier air at various locations in Cornwall (hence Geoffrey's inability to visit Birmingham when on leave in January 1916). Alice for some time seems to have moved between their house in Redditch, Warwickshire, and both Cornwall and London. Her dealings with the War Office were complicated by her frequent changes of address. By February 1919 Charles was dead.[11]

Edith's parents, James and Mary Ainscow, lived the productive life of a busy medical practice into the 1940s. They travelled extensively on the Continent and James publicly expressed his concern about the overriding military purpose, as he saw it, of the German *Autobahn* network under construction in the 1930s. He was also a passionate advocate of health service and social welfare reform. He, however, died (aged 70) in 1943 and Mary in 1947.

Edith died on 16th August 1983, but Wilfred, who was several years younger, outlived her by more than eight years. In March 1990 he became too frail to live any more on his own in the family home and went into a nursing home locally. He died at the age of 87 on 14th October 1991. From the end of March until some time in May 1990 I spent most of my time living in his house, sorting and clearing the contents, and preparing it for sale. There was no central heating, the ceilings in some rooms were collapsing, cobwebs were everywhere and the lounge suite was scarred with burn holes from my father's pipe. Neither of my parents had had much idea of throwing things away. It was the same house they had taken over at the time of their marriage in 1934, 56 years before. Wilfred had closed his dental practice 20 years earlier, but the surgery was still intact, together with all his dental tools and a variety of chemicals I had to dispose of. Not surprisingly, therefore, the house was full of reminders of my own childhood, and insights into aspects of their earlier life I had barely known. It contained also enormous quantities of junk, and I cannot now remember whether in the course of clearing it I filled five standard-sized skips or six. Regularly, I had people knocking at the door asking if they could retrieve scrap iron from them. I had frequent visits from a persistent 'antiques dealer', and 'prospective buyers' traipsing through the house, most of them just for the purposes of entertainment on a Saturday afternoon.

Discovery

Under one of the beds there was a large wooden chest which was locked. Keys were scattered in drawers all over the house. It took a long time but eventually I found the right one.

On 6th April 1990 I opened the chest. In it was what I came to recognise as Edith's treasure trove. It included an exquisite set of coffee cups that I had no memory of ever seeing before. There were newspapers recording major national and international events, going back to the death of Queen Victoria in 1901. There was a collection of beautiful teaspoons. Other treasures. And I found a nondescript cardboard box, which had contained Fuller's biscuits or cakes. Its dimensions were approximately seven and a half inches by five inches by three, and it was tied up with rough string. When I started to open it I had absolutely no idea what it might contain. Inside, tightly packed, I found the letters between Geoff and Edith. Hers were inside a coarse cloth wallet. In addition, there were two indistinct photos of them (?) in a canoe, Geoff's visiting card: (Mr C. G. Boothby, The South Staffordshire Reg't), some French 'saucy pictures' of scantily clad young ladies, two khaki handkerchiefs, one clean and ironed, the other deeply stained, perhaps with blood, or more likely with rust, and a newspaper cutting giving the casualty list in which he is reported as killed.

When I opened the first letter and saw what it was, it was as though I had suddenly found that the world was not at all as I had imagined it to be, and that I was going to have to learn a whole new way of understanding. If that sounds a strong statement, consider the following. In the course of emptying the many cupboards and drawers of that decrepit and draughty old house, I had come across a number of framed photos of Geoff in his army uniform, as well as various memorabilia of his parents. Indeed, I had been aware of these for a long time, but had always assumed they were present because of the long friendship between the two families, my mother's and his. It had never entered into my head as a conceivable possibility that there was more to the story than this. I was not remotely oriented to the idea that my mother had had such a tragic relationship when she was seventeen to eighteen. But then I found this humble cake box, and its contents created a completely new dimension to my knowledge of my mother, and thus, in a sense, the world.[12]

Later that day, I read through all the letters at a sitting. I was overwhelmed. I realised that I was reading about a love affair three-quarters of a century old, that my mother had died as an old woman a little less than seven years before, yet here were these intensely alive young people writing to each other across the miles, frustrated in their desire to meet, no doubt realising that their relationship was most likely doomed by the cynical logic of military bestiality. Why, I wondered, had I been so blind? Why had my mother never told me of what must have been the most unforgettable episode in her life? – Well, that I could understand, in the sense that she might have feared I might take it in the wrong way. But why, if she was not willing to tell me about it, did she leave the letters for me to find? – because she must have known that I would no doubt eventually find them. But from my point of view, having found them, I could never talk with her about what had happened.

I could never learn what she felt, how she coped, how their families coped, how the experience changed her. By the time I found the letters, my father's physical and mental condition had deteriorated too much for me to ask him whether he knew about her relationship with Geoffrey. I am pretty sure that he did, but I cannot be completely certain.

All these questions went around and around in my head, I began to realise that some things she had said, over a long period, might have had a double meaning, or had I missed hints she was dropping? Once, for instance, there was a discussion about a bereavement, and my sentiment that "over time it becomes easier to bear" elicited from her the emphatic response "I know". That "I know" had a strange intonation, and now took on for me a new and particular significance, as did her longstanding concern for the Boothby family, and even her emotional response to the 'Last Post'. I wondered whether her decision to take me to the Shropshire countryside during the early, dangerous, stages of the Second War (which I knew my father had never been happy about), was related to her sense of loss and consequent concern to protect her only child.

I became uncomfortably aware that, had Geoff survived, I might never have existed. Did I owe my life to the First World War? For a while that was a moral dilemma for me, but I came to terms with it with the realisation that the chances of any particular person being born are perhaps millions to one against. Indeed, I became fascinated with Geoff, his personality and his strategies for coping with the appalling situations he had to meet. In a curious way he feels like a close friend. As the early bravado and sense of adventure comes face to face with the reality of life in the trenches, he experiences mortal fear, which was no doubt new to him. How completely frank about his inner feelings he was being with Edith is hard to know. There are places where he seems to want to spare her the real truth, but in my opinion he mostly comes close to expressing what he is feeling. He is buoyed by feelings of patriotism and hatred for the enemy (in part, no doubt, taken from the contemporary ideology, in part, though, genuinely thought out). Does he ever think of German soldiers as men with families and girl friends much like his? Perhaps he does deep down, though there is no evidence for this in the letters, but to think such thoughts consciously, still more to express them, would make him doubt what he has to do and would sap his morale.[13] Nevertheless, it is a sobering thought that a young person as humane and well educated as Geoffrey could find himself in a state of mind where such hatred is embedded as part of his psychological condition. He is sustained by army discipline, a commonly understood organisational structure and by the comradeship of his fellow soldiers. Last but not least, he is encouraged and refreshed by the correspondence with Edith, and by this time the two of them seem to have been deeply in love. There is not the slightest hint of disillusionment leading to any degree of disloyalty to his country's cause. But plainly he is experiencing fear, the kind of corrosive fear that in extreme cases can lead to breakdown.

Had he survived, probably he would have kept his fear sufficiently in check, become a 'hardened officer', but we need to remind ourselves that he was just 21, and that is a young age to face the probability of death on a daily basis. One wonders, also, how he would have fared back in Birmingham in time of peace. Would he have resumed his medical course, a proposition he was dismissive of at one point? He was certainly a more stable and balanced personality than Arthur, but he would have faced trying and testing problems of re-adjustment.

Landscape in Flanders

In mid-December 2004 my wife Audrey and I, together with our friends Anna Jo and Michael Righton, both schoolteachers, drove to Flanders. Anna Jo regularly took school parties on battlefield tours, and knew the area well. We passed through the Flemish town of Ieper (Ypres) and out south-east about four kilometers along the Menin Road. We turned off left on a minor road and a short distance further on walked along a track up a rise to a monument in front of a wood still known as Railway Wood, though the railway is long since gone. It is an octagonal stone monument surmounted with a stone cross with metal sword that is a feature of many Allied cemeteries in the region. The following inscription covers three facets of the octagon:

Arthur Stockwin at the Cross

BENEATH THIS SPOT
LIE THE BODIES
OF AN OFFICER
THREE NCOS, AND
EIGHT MEN OF OR
ATTACHED TO THE
177TH TUNNELLING COMPANY
THE ROYAL ENGINEERS
WHO WERE KILLED
IN ACTION UNDER-
GROUND DURING THE
DEFENCE OF YPRES
BETWEEN NOVEMBER
1915 AND AUGUST 1917

Among the 12 names inscribed on the remaining five facets is included:

SECOND LIEUTENANT

C. G. BOOTHBY

A large-scale map (40 ft. = 1 inch) entitled 'No. 11 Workings' (see pp. 103 & 104) indicates that the tunnel was blown close to where the monument to Geoffrey and the others stands. He is probably buried not immediately below it, but the evidence suggests that he is not many yards away.[14]

Just behind the monument is a small area of woodland on top of the rise, the trees all having grown since the Great War, which ruined those that stood earlier. Whether the present wood is located exactly on the place the British soldiers knew as Railway Wood is open to debate, but it is certainly close. On the edge of the present wood remain a number of shell craters, full of water and serving as ponds for wildfowl. Less than two minutes' walk away is a monument to several hundred officers and men of the Liverpool Scottish, killed and wounded in an advance towards German lines across the field sloping down from the rise on 16th June 1915.

Looking across that field, brilliant white with frost under a deep blue sky, we could see the spires of Ieper on the horizon. The Great War reduced the whole town, including its cathedral and beautiful mediaeval Cloth Hall, to piles of rubble, but it was lovingly and painstakingly rebuilt afterwards. In the middle distance was a neat white farmhouse with a carefully shaped red tiled roof and gabled windows, surrounded by farm buildings including a long barn. The farm looked orderly, self-contained and tranquil. Not far behind it and off to the left were scattered houses and the occasional shop along the Menin Road, with stands of trees at intervals into the distance. Further towards the right was another small wood, privately owned, where we were told a blocked-off entrance to the tunnel complex still existed. It was a well-ordered, apparently prosperous, and seemingly untroubled agricultural landscape, where ordinary people made a good living with unspectacular pursuits.

Not visible, but not far away, was the site of a chateau totally destroyed by shelling, and nearby some truly enormous shell craters, also full of

Pond formed in a shell crater near the Cross

water. Just beyond it, somewhat incongruously, was a noisy fun fair. The many battlefield visitors need some light relief for their families, it seems. Again not visible from the Tunnellers' monument but distributed at various places along the Menin Road are Allied war cemeteries, with identical white headstones (without distinction of rank), commemorating the fallen, some named, some unidentified. We visited a number of war museums in the area, some modern and interactive, others chaotically stuffed with the detritus of war – shell cases and bits of metal, grenades, guns of all shapes and sizes, helmets, badges, mess tins, old photographs of blasted landscape and gruesome pictures of the wounded and dead that could not possibly be shown on television. Somehow, those museums that were the least organised or up to date gave a more graphic account of the reality of the war in Flanders than those that were carefully thought out according to the most modern principles.

The Menin Gate, rebuilt in 1927 at the edge of Ieper, is where the Menin Road begins. It is designed somewhat in the style of the Arc de Triomphe in Paris, and on its inner walls are chiselled the names of more than 56,000 men of Britain and Commonwealth countries missing in action in the Great War, whose remains were never found or never identified. We twice attended the ceremony that is held at 8.00 pm every evening of the year, when buglers play the Last Post, there is wreath laying and sometimes speeches. Given that it was mid-December and extremely cold, a surprising number of people were present. Battlefield tourism is of course now a significant element in the economy of the area, as visitors from far and wide gather to wonder at scenes of where the first fully industrialised war of modern times created industrialised mass slaughter of young men on both sides.[15] Among them, every year, is a party of boys from Clayesmore School, remembering the *thirty-nine* young men from the school who died in the Great War.

Justification?

Did Geoffrey die in vain? The question raises perplexing moral and political issues over which oceans of ink have been spilt. All I can do here is to point to a possible approach to an answer. At the broadest level, we can identify two opposing positions. The first would say that Geoffrey was a gallant and patriotic officer, who died in the service of his country, which was fighting a just war. The supreme sacrifice that he made was therefore fully justified because the aims for which he fought were just. The second position, however, is very different. It says that the warfare in which Geoffrey was involved fully demonstrated that war itself is an unacceptable evil. The slaughter, pain and destruction, the wiping out of virtually a whole generation of young men in several countries, could not possibly be justified as a price to pay for the aims of the nation-states involved.

Many criticisms can be and have been made of the unqualified patriotism entailed by the phrase 'my country right or wrong', where human morality is subordinated to a nationalist ethic. War creates an impetus for official propaganda dehumanising or demonising the enemy, since it is easier to kill those who you believe are inhuman or demonic than those you regard as ordinary human beings with families much like your own.[16] It is true that wars may solve political problems, but wars may also store up twice as much trouble for the future. John Keegan points out that one of the German survivors of the battles round Ypres was none other than Adolf Hitler, whose subsequent career was shaped by his experiences in the trenches.[17]

But it is only right to point out difficulties with the second position. It would be difficult to justify, or sell to a democratic electorate, the proposition that your country should not defend itself when attacked or when an attack is imminent. More altruism than is normally present in human populations would be needed to allow this. The undoubted fact that one country's defensive posture may be perceived as aggression by its potential enemy should not lead one to suppose that a non-violent response to aggression against your homeland is likely to be politically, or even morally, viable. Moreover, if we take Nazi performance as an example, the option of capitulation before Nazi aggression would hardly have led to a peaceful outcome, since for the Nazis war was a central feature of international policy. It is also as well to understand that there are circumstances where, to avoid war, it is necessary to prepare for it.[18]

Both positions, therefore, are problematic. War, nevertheless, remains in almost all circumstances an appalling solution. If war is the pursuit of diplomacy by other means, it is also a sign of diplomatic failure, and moreover, the failure of politics and political leaders. This is true even though the causes of wars are many and varied, and include demographic imbalances (real and perceived), ethnic and religious conflicts, violent and repressive dictators, economic and territorial disputes and legacies from long-remembered historical wrongs.

This points us towards solutions that transcend the national level. In a sense the history of the past century has been one of search for an international political architecture that would render wars obsolete, or at least to limit their incidence. This search has been fitful, and often gives a sense of 'one step forward, two steps back'. Even so, progress has been made, as with the construction of the European Union, which, whatever its difficulties, has succeeded in rendering war between Germany and its neighbours close to impossible. The nature of war is, of course, not static, so that international stability may be threatened by new weapons systems and types of aggression. The causes of war also vary over time. But the responsibility of those in charge of human destinies to treat war as a last resort is arguably the gravest of all.

To return, therefore, to our question: did Geoffrey die in vain? It is difficult to avoid an answer starting 'on the one hand, on the other hand'. On the one hand, according to the prevailing ideology of the time among the Allied Powers (and which he shared), he was fighting to defend his country and to repel unprovoked aggression. On the other hand, practically all accounts of fighting on the Western front between 1914 and 1918 show such appalling conditions and levels of savagery that his death and that of so many others may be seen as such a waste of human life as to weigh heavily in the balance against the 'defence of country' argument. A cynic – I forget who – once described the Great War as 'a war to decide who controlled Strasbourg'. But much more was at stake than that, including who should be the predominant power in Europe. There is, however, a kernel of truth even in such a cynical statement, namely that the human cost of possibly laudable political objectives was horrifyingly high.

It is thus impossible to answer our question in a really satisfactory way (though readers will no doubt have strong opinions, one way or the other). My own answer is that his death represents a damnable consequence of monstrous political failure on an international scale.[19] But at the same time I believe we owe more than it is now easy to imagine to Geoffrey and those like him – ordinary men on all sides of the war – who, thrown into the maelstrom, acted in a fashion that could attract a number of adjectives. The one I choose is 'awe-inspiring'. And we owe much also to their families, who had to live on and cope with the war's baleful consequences. Our generation owes it to his and their memory to create and develop international structures robust enough to ensure that he did not die in vain.

Notes

1. This is presumably the officer just senior to Geoffrey, who was awarded a decoration instead of him, according to Major Raper's letter to Alice Boothby quoted above.
2. *Clayesmorian*, December 1916, pp. 127–8
3. See Glossary
4. *Clayesmorian*, April 1916, p. 66
5. From the dated photograph mentioned above, it is clear that he left a day or two before the 19th.

6. Diary of 172 RE Coy, National Archives file WO 95/244, entry for 21st August 1915.

7. *Ibid.*, entry for 5th October 1915

8. Letter of 4th November 1915

9. National Archives, file WO95/404

10. In the 1930s she wrote occasional articles on child health in the local press, For instance during a national health campaign in 1937 she wrote a two-part article entitled "The Toddler" in the *Smethwick Telephone*, part 1, date uncertain, part 2, 11th December 1937.

11. Letter from Alice Boothby to the War Office, 17th February 1919. National Archives File WO339/5068

12. The intensity of my response was also undoubtedly enhanced by the fact that we had lost our younger son, Tim, in a skiing accident in December 1987, rather more than two years earlier. I wrote about him in *The Story of Tim*. Richmond, Surrey, Curzon Press, 1993. Copies are available from the editor of the present volume: arthur.stockwin@sant.ox.ac.uk

13. "The underground war was principally one of stealth; a deadly game in which both attacker and attacked sought to outwit their opponent, predicting their movements without giving away their own positions – and killing without compunction, emotion or hesitation. There was no room for chivalry or mercy in mine warfare; it was kill or be killed." Peter Barton, Peter Doyle and Johan Vanderwalle, *Beneath Flanders Fields: The Tunnellers' War, 1914-1918*. Staplehurst: Spellmount, 2004, p. 97

14. "No. 11 Workings. Scale:- 40' = 1" Signed M.J. Wilkinson, Capt. R.E., for Major, R.E., O.C. 177th Tunnelling Coy. R.E. The map was kindly supplied by Peter Barton.

15. We should not forget that the slaughter was not on one side only. Some eight km. north of Ieper is the German cemetery at Langemarck. John Keegan writes graphically about it, saying that in October 1914 large numbers of almost untrained conscripts from German universities "after two months of drill, were thrown into action against the regulars of the British army near Ypres in Belgium. The result was a massacre of the innocents (known in Germany as the *Kindermord bei Ypern*), of which a ghastly memorial can be seen to this day. In the Langemarck cemetery, overlooked by a shrine decorated by the insignia of Germany's universities, lie the bodies of 36,000 young men interred in a common grave, all killed in three weeks of fighting; the number almost equals that of the United States' battle casualties in seven years of war in Vietnam." John Keegan, *A History of Warfare*. London: Hutchinson, 1993, pp. 358–9.

16. See John Dower, *War without Mercy: Race and Power in the Pacific War*. London, Faber and Faber, 1986. American cartoonists in the war often portrayed Japanese as monkeys or as ogres, while Japanese cartoonists showed Americans as fat slobs, bloated capitalists etc. One cartoon reproduced in the book shows a Japanese woman combing her hair to get rid of "American dandruff" (p. 191)

17. Keegan, p. 359.

18. Preparation for war, however, does not always result in its avoidance, as the outbreak of the Great War graphically shows

19. I will pass on the question, which has much occupied historians, how far political and military failures at the national level contributed to the military impasse on the Western front and the consequent slaughter.

Acknowledgements

I am grateful to my family for supporting this project. In particular my son Rupert has, with expertise that I lack, combed the Internet for relevant material and has also helped with ideas for cover design. My wife Audrey has given me moral support and acted as a sounding board for my talk about the letters, ever since I discovered them in 1990. I owe a particular debt to Anna Jo Righton, who helped with her expertise about West Flanders from taking school parties on battlefield tours, and who, with Michael Righton, made the arrangements for our trip to Ieper in December 2004. She proved to be a whizz with a computer, turning up interesting material (particularly about Geoffrey's family) on the Internet. And Michael I thank for his photographs of the area on pages 3, 116 and 118 and also on the cover. Our daughter Kate and son-in-law Michael, and daughter Jane and son-in-law Russell, have also encouraged me. Rikki Kersten of the University of Leiden, knowledgeable about war literature, gave me useful advice and encouragement when I spoke with her in Tokyo in January 2005. My thanks also to Tony Chew, history master at Clayesmore School, who, on a school trip to the battlefields at Christmas 2003, laid a wreath at the monument at Railway Wood to former pupil, Geoffrey Boothby.

While at Ieper we visited a bookshop and bought a copy of the magnificent book on Great War tunnelling by Peter Barton, Peter Doyle and Johan Vandewalle, *Beneath Flanders Fields,* (see Further Reading). We then found our way to Johan Vandewalle's restaurant, 'De Dreve', at Polygon Wood, and, over a tasty lunch, talked with him about the tunnels, which he has extensively explored. His expertise is particularly relevant locally because there are cases of houses collapsing into the rabbit warren of passages that remain under West Flanders. He also put me in touch with his co-author Peter Barton, of Parapet Productions, who has been enormously helpful in providing maps of the tunnels and in guiding me through files at the National Archives. The day I spent with him there in February 2005 was exciting and memorable. I am also indebted to Roderick Suddaby, who found me useful material at the Imperial War Museum.

I thank the Morton Media Group for their kind permission to reproduce the photograph of the Hudson motorbike on p. 21 and the Royal Engineers Library for allowing us to use the maps on pages 103 and 104. I must also thank the National Archives for permission to reproduce various documents in their collection.

I am grateful to Amanda Helm, whom I met in the summer of 2004 and told about the letters, for suggesting my publisher, and for doing the typesetting. And I have a particular debt of gratitude to the Parapress team for making it possible for the letters between Geoffrey Boothby and Edith Ainscow to see the light of day.

And last but not least, I find it hard to find words to thank those two young people who, nine-tenths of a century ago, were writing life-enhancing letters to each other that reverberate down the years.

Further Reading

There are many, many books on the First World War, and the following is a short selection that may be of particular interest to readers.

The best and most up-to-date book on tunnelling, by three experts who have devoted many years to its study, is the following work, lavishly illustrated with photographs (some in colour), maps of tunnel systems and line drawings:

Peter Barton, Peter Doyle and Johan Vanderwalle, *Beneath Flanders Fields: The Tunnellers' War 1914-1918*. Staplehurst: Spellmount, 2004.

A much earlier work, written while many survivors of the tunnelling war were alive and still relatively young, was:

Capt. W. Grant Grieve and Bernard Newman, *Tunnellers*. London: Herbert Jenkins Ltd., 1936 (There is a Naval and Military Press reprint).

See also:

Alexander Barrie, *War Underground*, New York: Ballantine Books, 1961; Staplehurst, Kent: Spellmount, 2000

General books on the Great War come with many different perspectives and emphases. The following is a small selection of accessible single-volume works:

Correlli Barnett, *The Great War*. London: BBC Worldwide, 2nd edn, 2003.
Niall Ferguson, *The Pity of War*. London: Penguin, 1999.
James Joll, *The Origins of the First World War*. Harlow, Essex, Longman, 1984.

John Keegan, *A History of Warfare*. London: Hutchinson, 1993, a general analysis by a fine historian that places wars of the 20th century in context.

Keith Robbins, *The First World War*. Oxford: Oxford University Press, 2nd edn, 2002.

John Turner (ed.), *Britain and the First World War*. London: Unwin Hyman, 1988.

Denis Winter, *Death's Men: Soldiers of the Great War*. London: Penguin, 1992.

Books or booklets giving detailed information about the battles and battle-lines in the Ypres salient are most readily available in the bookshop of the National Archives near Kew Gardens, Surrey, the Imperial War Museum on Lambeth Road, London, and also at the "In Flanders Fields" Museum in the Cloth Hall at Ieper (Ypres). A brief selection follows, including an item of battlefield archaeology:

Battlefield Europe series includes the following:

Nigel Cave, *Polygon Wood*. Barnsley, South Yorks: Leo Cooper, Pen and Sword Books, 1999.

Paul Reed, *Walking the Salient*. Barnsley, South Yorks: Leo Cooper, Pen and Sword Books, latest edn 2004. (Includes a most useful bibliography.)

Other short books in the series are: *Sanctuary Wood and Hooge, Passchendaele, St Julien, Hill 60, Messines*, as well as others relating to the Somme, etc.

Malcolm Hall, *In Enemy Hands: A British Territorial Soldier in Germany 1915–1919*. Stroud, Glos.: Tempus Publishing, 2002. (This concerns a soldier captured by the Germans close to Ieper in 1915. Although much of it describes his time in captivity in Germany, there are also graphic descriptions of the fighting that he experienced, and some fine photographs).

J. Giles, *Flanders Then and Now: The Ypres Salient and Passchendaele*. Third revised and re-titled edn of a 1979 book originally titled *The Ypres Salient Then and Now*. London: After the Battle Books, 2004 (?). See www.afterthebattle.com.

Tonie and Valmai Holt, *Major and Mrs. Holt's Battle Map of the Ypres Salient*, Sandwich, Kent: T. and V. Holt Associates, 1996.

Mathieu de Meyer and Pedro Pype, with an Introduction by Marc Dewilde,

The A19 Project: Archaeological Research at Cross Roads, Zarren, Belgium: Association for World War Archaeology, 2004, (website: www.a-w-a.be).

Finally, we should not neglect the fact that the horrors of fighting on the Western Front inspired some of the most remarkable and moving English literature of modern times. Two much quoted poems encapsulate the pathos of the events: "In Flanders Fields", by John McCrae, and "Perhaps (to R.A.L.)", by Vera Britain. But for my money the most profound poem from the war is Wilfred Owen's "Strange Meeting", with its haunting line "I am the enemy you killed, my friend". In "Dulce et decorum est" Owen - by all accounts a brave officer - relates the effects of a gas attack and draws a searing conclusion about a time-honoured mantra going all the way back to the Roman Empire, glorifying service in war. And in "Exposure", he penetrates the psychology of men in the trenches, caught in some kind of unreal existence of boredom, dreams and sudden death, culminating in the line: "But nothing happens." Similar greatness attaches to Siegfried Sassoon, a graphic word-artist who portrays the butchery of war and its consequences with a savage and at times satirical eye, as in the poem "Does it matter?", or in "Base Details". A fine collection of such poems and many more is the following:

Jon Silkin (ed.), *The Penguin Book of First World War Poetry.* 2nd edn, revised, 1996

For Owen fans (like me), see also:

Jon Stallworthy (ed.), *The Poems of Wilfred Owen.* London: Hogarth Press, 1987

The best selling novel, *Birdsong* by Sebastian Faulks, perhaps more than any history book, aroused a widespread interest in the tunnels and tunnellers of the Great War. Even though it transferred certain tunnelling techniques such as "clay-kicking" from Flanders to much further down the line in France (where the geology was different),[1] it is literally accurate about much of what happened in the tunnels. Literary experts and ordinary readers may differ on its merits as a novel. Nevertheless, it creates a hellish and fascinating world of death, madness and bravery utterly different from the experiences of most people alive today.

Sebastian Faulks, *Birdsong*. London: Random House (Vintage), 1994.

Note

1.   I am grateful to Peter Barton for this information.

Glossary of Terms and Abbreviations

Archies	Artillerymen
Batt., Batt'n	Battalion
Bde.	Brigade
B.E.F.	British Expeditionary Force
Bosch, Bosche	German (derogatory)
Camberley	the Camberley Staff College, for officer training
camouflet	snub (French): an explosive charge designed to destroy a subterranean gallery in the hands of the enemy
cheval de frise	barbed wire entanglements (French)
cotidie	every day (Latin, correct spelling 'quotidie')
Coy.	Company
crump	explosion
cum grano salis	with a grain of salt (Latin)
dernier cri	the very latest fashion (French)
D.S.O.	Distinguished Service Order
D.V.	Deo volente (Latin): God willing
flapper up	a young girl who has not yet put her hair up
Harlene	a kind of shampoo that was supposed to stop hair falling out
Hun	German (derogatory)
Kitchener's Army	an army of civilian volunteers mobilised by Lord Kitchener, amounting to 1,186,337 men by the end of 1914, and 2,257,521 by September 1915.[1]
knut	a dandy
Medit. E.F.	Mediterranean Expeditionary Force (from late in 1915 also often called the Dardanelles Army)
occifer	officer (slang)
orficer	officer (slang)
pro.tem.	pro tempore (Latin): for the time being

R.A.M.C.	Royal Army Medical Corps
R.E.	Royal Engineers
Regt.	Regiment
sap	a narrow communicating trench
sapper	a private of the Royal Engineers
strafe	as verb: to punish (German), to do damage to, to attack fiercely. As noun: fierce assault, a period of heavy shelling.
sub., subaltern	an army officer of rank below that of captain
Suvla Bay	site of the allied withdrawal from Gallipoli
thusness	"a state of being thus"
tranchées	trenches (French)
unten	underneath, below (German)
vide hoc	see this (Latin)
Zep.	Zeppelin

Note

1. Correlli Barnett, *The Great War*. London: BBC Worldwide, 2003, pp. 55–6.